Alaskan Adventure

By Frederick James Currier

An
Alaskan Adventure

A Story of Finding Gold in the Far North

From: 1894-1903

By Frederick James Currier

Foreword by Randy Zarnke

Edited By
Amy June Currier Jorgensen

PUBLICATION
CONSULTANTS
We Believe In The Power Of Authors

PO Box 221974 Anchorage, Alaska 99522-1974
books@publicationconsultants.com www.publicationconsultants.com

ISBN Number: 978-1-59433-843-4
eBook ISBN Number: 978-1-59433-844-1

Library of Congress Catalog Card Number: 2018962723

Manufactured in the United States of America

Dedication

This book is dedicated to Frederick James Currier and all the intrepid pioneers who journeyed north to the Great Land. They lived a life of adventure, even if they did not all find their fortunes.

Contents

Chapters

Biographical sketch of Frederick James Currier

Frederick James Currier was born on February 13, 1860 in River Falls, Wisconsin to James Kimball Currier and Florilla Locke Currier. He had two younger sisters, Mary Louise and Lillian, and a brother, Harry.

Frederick was always a young man looking for adventure. He loved the outdoors, camping, fishing, and hiking. He was a graduate of River Falls Normal School, majoring in natural sciences. He married Abbie M. Parker of River Falls on June 24, 1885, when he was 25 and she was 22. They had five children: Gladys, Ruth, Donald, Maxwell, and Geneva. The two older children were born in River Falls, and the others were born in Turton, South Dakota, where the family moved to a wheat and stock farm in 1888. In 1893 the family returned to River Falls, leasing the farm in South Dakota, so the older children could be entered in the primary schools and have better educational advantages than were offered in the Dakota territory.

In March of 1894, Fred J. Currier went by way of the Canadian Pacific Railroad to Vancouver, B.C., intending to go down into Oregon to purchase an apple orchard and then move his family out there. Instead, he met two miners in a hotel in Victoria who were about to depart on a trip into the interior of Alaska to seek gold. They showed Fred J. nuggets and invited him to accompany them. Fred accepted, forgetting the apple orchard idea. His "memoirs" cover the next decade of his adventures as he sought "his fortune" in the gold fields.

In 1904, he moved his family to the Santa Clara Valley of California, settling in Saratoga where he purchased a prune orchard. The children completed their education in the local schools, with Donald and Ruth later attending Stanford University in Palo Alto, Max going to a mechanical engineering school in San Francisco, and Gladys and Geneva attending San Jose State Normal School.

Fred's first wife, Abbie, died in 1908 and is interred in Madronia Cemetery in Saratoga. Fred's oldest daughter, Gladys, kept house and looked after the family for the next ten years. In 1913, Ruth married Paul W. Merrill who later became an eminent astronomer at Mt. Wilson observatory in Pasadena, California. A crater on the moon is named after him. Max married Emily Van Hovenberg in 1914; Geneva married Leland Huntington in 1917; and Gladys married James Law in 1918. Donald served in World War I and married Louise Hallmeyer in 1929. All these children are deceased.

Just before Gladys married, Frederick James Currier married Jennie (Jean) B. Smith of Saratoga on April 10, 1918. They honeymooned in various California beauty spots for six months. Fred then accepted a position as manager of the

California Prune and Apricot Growers packing house in Red Bluff, California. (He had sold his prune orchard in the Santa Clara valley before his second marriage.) A daughter, Amy June, was born to Jean and Fred on June 11, 1920.

In 1929 the Currier family returned to Saratoga and built a beautiful home on a five-acre wooded estate which they called "Brookbanks" as the Saratoga Creek ran through the property. They also purchased a prune orchard adjoining the property and Fred went back to ranching for the next six years, until his death on November 25, 1935. His death was the result of a blood clot in the pulmonary artery of the heart after abdominal surgery. He was 75 years old when he died. He is interred in Madronia Cemetery, Saratoga. His second wife, Jean, died in 1971 at the age of 90, and is inurned in Madronia Cemetery also.

There are six grandchildren: Emily Currier Hall, Gordon Leland Huntington, Donald Huntington Merrill, Kirke Currier Jorgensen, Locke Currier Jorgensen, and Rilla Jorgensen Betz, all of whom live in the state of California, the three latter being the children of Amy June Currier and her husband, Colonel John G. Jorgensen, whom she married on May 22, 1943.

At present, there are nine great-grandchildren of Frederick James Currier and several great-great grandchildren.

Frederick Currier on the left.

Foreword

The manuscript for this book was written by Frederick James Currier and edited by his daughter Amy June Currier Jorgensen. It tells the story of Frederick's adventures in Alaska from 1894 – 1903. Most of the tales take place in Interior Alaska, with some trips up and down the Yukon River.

I first saw a copy of this manuscript in 2007. I was immediately impressed by both the level of adventure and quality of writing. I can't claim to have read every Alaskan adventure book, but I have read most of them. Frederick's *Alaskan Adventure* compares favorably with the best of this genre.

I shared that original manuscript with a couple friends. They both affirmed my assessment. I concluded that we had to find a way to share this great story with other readers who have similar interests. The first step was obtaining permission from the family. Locating any of Frederick's heirs proved to be a challenge. Once I contacted his grandson Kirke Jorgensen, he granted approval to move ahead with the project.

The next step was finding some images to augment the text. My good friend Marty Meierotto took me to the small community of Central, Alaska, where we met with Laurel Tyrrell and Al Cook. These folks manage the Circle District Historical Sociatey. Among other things, the Museum contains lots of historic photographs, many of which are from the same time period as Currier's adventures. Thanks to the generosity of Laurel and Al, you will see numerous Museum photos in this book. Justin Maple created several maps for the book, which should add to the readers' experience. Ryan Ragan deserves credit for the lay-out and design of the book.

Currier's manuscript contained no mention of the amount of gold that his hard labor produced in Alaska. However, we must assume that he was a successful miner. He had a large boat built specifically for plying the rivers of our State. When he left Alaska, he bought a large tract of land in California. Those are both signs of a successful miner. He demonstrated a commitment to his mining endeavors, which made him successful. I suspect that Currier valued the friendships he forged along the way just as much as he valued the financial rewards.

I admire the men and women who explored and settled Alaska. I am in awe of their fortitude, work ethic and sense of adventure. I have the utmost respect for the hardships they endured. I am grateful to Frederick Currier for documenting his adventures in our State. This finished book is a fitting memorial to the man. The book is long overdue, but according to the old cliché ... "Better late than never."

The Alaska Trappers Association is proud to share this outstanding book with our friends around the world. We hope that you enjoy reading it as much as we did.

~ By Randy Zarnke

Chapter 1

Apples of Gold

"Come out to Oregon and buy an apple orchard," so wrote my cousin Rossie in the winter of 1893. My family and I had just returned from the Dakotas where we had been living during the past seven years on a grain and stock ranch. Our children, five in number, were reaching an age where they needed better school and church privileges than the newly opened territory provided. Accordingly, we had leased our ranch and stock to a neighbor and returned to River Falls, Wisconsin, to take advantages of the fine schools that the town possessed. The children's maternal grandmother lived in the town and my parents were on a farm but a short distance away. We purchased a home within easy distance to the Normal School building and entered the older children in the primary and intermediate departments of the school.

After we were nicely settled for the winter, I began to wonder what I would do with myself while the children were in school. Then came the letter from cousin Rossie and it at once appealed to me as a wise move. I would go to Oregon, start an apple orchard, and when I had it in a thriving condition bring out the family.

The newly opened Canadian Pacific Railroad was at this time calling the attention of the public to the vast fertile prairies, the wonderful forests and coal lands in the Rockies and Selkirks, and dwelling in vivid word pictures on the beauties of the lakes, glaciers, and waterfalls along the route. Eager to see these attractions, I secured my transportation to the coast over this line.

Leaving the ice and snow of Wisconsin and Minnesota in March of 1894, our train crossed the latter state, stretching out northwest ward toward Canada, and the rail line met the Canadian Pacific at Moosejaw, which was nothing at that time but a junction on the bleak, unsettled plains of Manitoba, several hundred miles west of Winnipeg. While I was waiting at Moosejaw for connections on the prairie line, a freight train from Kansas pulled into the station. The whole train had been chartered by one man. With his snow white hair, long beard and patriarchal look he reminded me of Abraham moving

12

to the promised land! He had sixty people in his train ~ sons, grandsons, and great-grandsons with their families and all their household goods and cattle. They were moving to a ten thousand acre concession that the patriarch had obtained in Alberta province some hundred miles west of Moosejaw. The Canadian Pacific was eager to get reliable settlers from the United States at this time and was making very liberal concessions to them.

A day's rather monotonous travel over the plains of Manitoba and Saskatchewan brought us to the Rockies and from there on until we reached the coast we were never out of sight of snow capped peaks and glaciers. The Selkirks were especially awe-inspiring and then came the run down the Fraser Canyon until we finally pulled into Vancouver, the terminus of the line. Stumps, stumps, nothing but stumps was my first impression of that town! I was told it took forty days for a man to dig out one stump, and I could well believe it, and yet in a few more years all those stump-covered hills were to be lined with homes and stores and factories.

From Vancouver I planned to go south via Seattle and Tacoma to Roseburg to join cousin Rossie, but noticing a steamer at the wharf that was leaving for Victoria, I decided to see that old English city first. A night's ride across the Straits of Georgia and we were in the land-locked harbor of Victoria with its rocky shores and heavily timbered slopes. The morning air was warm and balmy, filled with fragrance of fresh earth, green grass and flowering shrubs. A walk around the town amazed me! Such a luxuriance of flowers prevailed everywhere. And this was March! A week ago I had left ice and snow and here were roses, violets, tulips, and scores of flowers and shrubs new to me that met the eye on every hand. But one must eat and at the hotel where I went for that purpose and to secure a room for the night I met my fate, or at least I met conditions that led me on quite a different path from the one I had planned on taking.

At the table where I ate were two weather-beaten hardy Cassiar miners, George McCue and George White. With White was his nephew, Bob White. From this conversation I learned that the party was bound for the Yukon to the newly discovered placer diggings on Forty Mile. George McCue had

13

returned from there the fall before. He was the discoverer of Franklin Gulch on the Forty Mile River. Up to the time of his discovery of placer gold, there had been a little spasmodic bar mining on several rivers. Cassiar Bar on the Lewes, some bars on Stewart River, and Bonanza Bar on Forty Mile had attracted prospectors who would cross the range in the spring, pan a little during low water in the summer, then return to the outside to winter. But with the discovery of placer gold on the Forty Mile there was to be quite a rush into that locality this coming season. In fact, the steamer *City of Topeka* was now loading at the wharf due to leave for Juneau in the morning. I was greatly interested in the talk and we all adjourned to the smoking room after dinner where McCue gave us more particulars about the country, the trip in, and then produced his poke (buckskin bag) and poured out a handful of nuggets he had taken out of his claim the season before.

Of course nuggets of gold were an old story to George White, but to Bob and me our first sight of nature's gold was a fascinating spectacle. I made many eager inquiries as to methods of getting into that country and my breath was fairly taken away when McCue gave me an invitation to join them on the trip in.

"But I have no outfit," I exclaimed.

"You don't need any," said McCue. "Get aboard in the morning and we will outfit at Juneau."

"That's fine of you, gentlemen," I replied. "I will be with you!"

Forgotten were cousin Rossie and the apple orchard in Oregon! I dreamed of gold nuggets as big as yellow pumpkins that night. I wrote home telling my wife, Abbie, of my change of plans and advised her to tell all the relatives and to send letters to Forty Mile. I did not realize that it would be over a year before it would be possible for letters to reach me there!

Chapter 2
The Inland Passage

Bright and early we were aboard the steamer and northward bound. This was to be a wonderful week. All up the British Columbia coast and then along Alaska is a sunken mountain range (the Coast Range of California.) The tops of the sunken range form thousands of islands and between them and the mainland is a thousand miles of protected waterway. Some places had widened out in lake-like expanse and other spots had contracted to narrow river-like channels, but always the steamer forged ahead, one channel leading to another and all protected from the storm-tossed ocean. At the time I first traveled this Inland Passage only a few adventurous steamers plowed its unchartered and unlighted course, but today it is one of the most popular summer excursion trips.

The islands rise sheer from the water's edge, heavily timbered with a valuable cedar from which the Indians make their celebrated canoes, some of which are seventy feet long, capable of carrying thirty people. Here at the Indian villages we saw the totem poles with their grotesque carvings. Some of the totems are sixty or seventy feet high. The carvings, representatives of the bear, wolf, raven, whale or other animal, are really records of the family tree, so one who is expert in the clan nomenclature can trace the genealogy of the family by studying the totem pole standing before the house door.

On the way I made the acquaintance of Father William Duncan who was the missionary to a tribe of Indians on New Metlakatla Island. Father Duncan had taken the tribe to this island, built a school and church, established a sawmill and cannery and built up a prosperous and self-sustaining community. He told me that he had had to hang a few of their witch doctors in the early years, but that now all the tribe were Christians. As the boat pulled into the landing of this island, a uniformed brass band came down and gave a very creditable exhibition.

When the steward had assigned my berth on the *City of Topeka* he had put me in a cabin with two other occupants, Ralph and Alex Thayer from Duluth, Minnesota. Later, when we were all together with McCue and White, McCue suggested that the Thayers join us and make a party of six.

"We can help each other across the range and in building boats on the river," he explained. "Then when we get to Forty Mile we can split up again and each one be on his own."

That suited the Thayer boys and of course I was agreeable as McCue knew the ropes much better than anyone else, having made two trips in before this one.

Lt. W. Ogilvie and a party of surveyors were aboard the steamer also, bound for Juneau, where they were to begin the boundary survey between Alaska and Canada. This boundary line had been a source of dispute between Great Britain and the United States. Under the Russian treaty, the line starting at Wrangell was to parallel the coast at a distance of twenty miles until it reached the 141 meridian and thence north along that line to the Arctic. As the shoreline from Wrangell north along the inland waterway we were following was indented with many deep, river-like inlets or fjords, some of them running back one hundred miles or more, it necessarily made a very circuitous line. Great Britain claimed that the boundary line should stretch from headland to headland, cutting across these fjords. The United States (and she was backed by Russia) claimed the treaty called for a line twenty miles back from saltwater. This contention cut Great Britain off entirely from a seaport north of Wrangell. The dispute settled by arbitration sustained the position held by the United States and Russia. It was the object of Lt. Ogilvie and his party to now locate this line. (Under the decision, Juneau, Dyea, and Skagway were in the United States.)

Off Taku Arm we encountered the first icebergs. Huge blocks of ice had broken off from Taku Glacier. The steamer slowed up and hoisted aboard several blocks of ice to replenish her iceboxes, and some natives came alongside with their canoes and offered fresh halibut for sale. I saw the steward purchase one weighing one hundred pounds for $1.00. Several of the fish had great slices torn out of their sides. The fishermen explained this was done by seals that would dash in and cut out a mouthful as the fish were being drawn up from the deep when they were hooked. These seals were the fur seals, now on their annual northern migration to their breeding grounds in the Bering Sea.

A long, melodious whistle and the *City of Topeka* drew up Gastineau Channel and tied up at the wharf at Juneau. Alex commented that it looked as if the town might slide off any minute into the sea. Perched on a steep hillside with the dark, fir-clad mountain overhanging it, it certainly did appear like a perilous location for a city.

Across the channel, a mile away, was Douglas Island. On this was the Treadwell Mine which had produced over forty million dollars of gold. The Thayer boys and I took occasion the following day to run across and see the famous mine. It was an immense open cut or quarry, quite different from my idea of a quartz mine. The ore was very low grade, only $1.60 per ton, but the "body" was so immense that the quantity, handled cheaply under the open cut method, gave a handsome profit. In later years as the cut was deepened and carried under the ocean bed, the saltwater finally broke through and flooded the mine and destroyed it.

"All off," called McCue. "Better find a place to sleep for we will be a few days getting our outfit together."

There was not much in hotel accommodations, we discovered. Ogilvie and party had filled the only hotel, but we finally located a couple of bedrooms in a private home.

"Now for our outfit," explained McCue. "We want only just enough to take us in. Any extra pound that is unnecessary will hold us back just that much."

He looked at our store clothes, white shirts, collars and said, "Better dump all those things and get an outfit fit for the trail."

At the outfitting store of Green and Bro. we purchased woolen shirts, mackinaw coats and trousers, moccasins, gum boots, mittens and headgear.

"Put all your outgoing togs in your suitcases and store them in my attic," offered Mr. Green. "Then when you come back to go outside you can pick them up."

In the attic where we finally left our suitcases were a hundred or more other cases, bundles, and boxes all piled helter-skelter. It looked like a rather risky proposition to leave anything valuable there and expect to claim it again. Anyone returning was told to go up attic and pick out his belongings. If he could not find his own maybe someone else's would do instead! However, as I never returned that way I was not troubled on any futile search for my own suitcase. It may be there yet for all I know!

Our personal outfits secured, we next turned to the needs of the trail. Here we left it entirely to McCue.

"First we want two sleds," he directed.

These were of the well-known Yukon make, eight feet long, eighteen inches wide, twelve inches high, oak frame with steel runners, a gee pole and pulling rope. This style was well suited for the trail and is used to this day over the

Northwest. A seven-foot whipsaw, handsaw, plane, ax, hammer, nails, auger, pitch and oakum were items needed for boat-building. A Yukon stove of sheet iron with the necessary cooking utensils, plates, knives and forks was next on the list. Then there was a twelve-by-fourteen foot tarpaulin for shelter. Our grocery list included 150 pounds of flour, 40 pounds of beans, 100 pounds of bacon, 20 pounds of sugar, 5 pounds of coffee, a bag of salt, 5 pounds of butter, baking powder, and 10 pounds of rice.

"There," said McCue with satisfaction, "that will see us through, and it makes near 400 pounds to each sled. That's a load enough by the time we get it over the pass."

A small tug was loading for the run up the Lynn Canal from Juneau to Dyea, 110 miles away. A score of other prospectors and their outfits were loading and our party completed the load. A head wind was blowing and the heavily laden vessel made slow progress up the canal. Mount Fairweather with its enormous glacier was sending cold boreal blasts down upon us. The whitecaps splashed over the bow of the tug as it forced its way onward. Eighty miles up the canal were two forks. The left hand channel led to Dyea, our destination; the right hand channel led to where Skagway was later to be located.

"Here we are," shouted McCue as the tug dropped anchor a mile from the ice-boarded mudflat at the end of our trip. Several scows came alongside and the work of unloading was rushed forward. Everyone was in a hurry and the utmost confusion prevailed. Outfits were inextricably mixed and more than one heated dispute arose between rival claimants.

"Here you fellows," called McCue to us. "Stand here and grab our stuff as it comes up out of the hold. We will get it all together on one scow so there will be no mix-up on the shore."

Our stuff was plainly marked and as sling-load after sling-load came up and was dumped on the deck, we watched our chance and rushed in and grabbed each article or box we could identify. Alex had the list and checked off the items as we secured them. When he declared it all accounted for, McCue ordered, "Now there, you scow men! Alongside here and take this stuff!"

We piled it over the side to the scow and than all six of us got aboard.

"Light out for the shore now," ordered McCue.

"It will cost you $30.00 if I don't take on any more cargo," argued the boatman.

"All right, here is your money," said McCue. "Now pull for it."

We all turned in with oars and paddles and later, as the water grew shallow, with poles and pushed the scow up alongside the ice sheet. Outfits were being piled up and scattered along the shore in all directions.

"Dozens of them will get soaked when the tide comes in if they don't get a move on," commented McCue.

Loading our outfits on our sleds and attaching the draw ropes, we started for the fringe of timber a mile across the tide flats. Here was the mouth of the Dyea River, a rushing, brawling stream fed by the glaciers and snow slopes of the towering mountains. A trading post run by Capt. John J. Healy was here where barter was carried on with the interior Stick Indians. A village of these latter was located nearby.

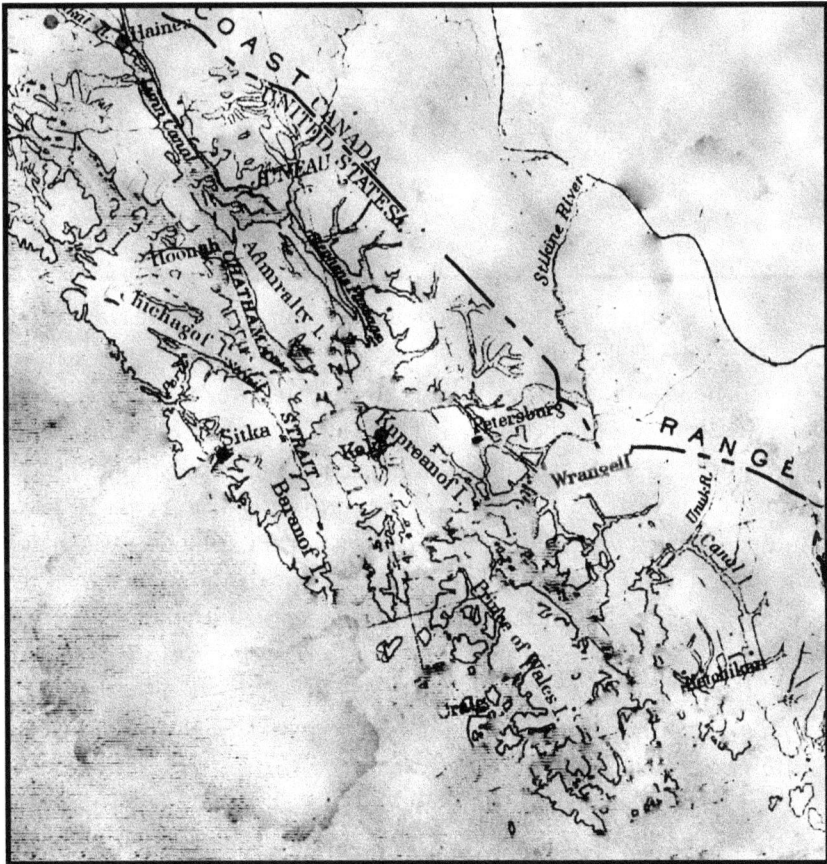

Southeast Alaska.

Chapter 3

The Chilkoot Trail

Packers Ascending Summit of Chilkoot Pass, May, 1898.

"We will need some of the Indians to help us over the pass," explained McCue. Now, how are you boys fixed? There are two ways of getting over. If you have plenty of money we can hire packers right from here to Lake Lindeman, or we can get our stuff up to Sheep Camp and just get the Sticks to pack it to the summit. The first way will cost fifty cents a pound, the other way half that."

Neither the Thayer boys nor I had any too much money and we wanted to go as cheaply as we could. McCue was agreeable either way. We learned at the trading post that travel had been held up at the summit for a week by constant blizzards.

We made our first camp that night on the banks of the Dyea River. The tarpaulin was stretched up as a lean-to facing a roaring fire of drift logs, and a bed of spruce boughs was spread down on which to pile our bedding. Alex essayed the office of chief cook. The Yukon stove was set up. The telescope pipe of three lengths was added and when filled with kindling and dry wood the stove drew beautifully. In fact, we never had any difficulty with the stove whenever any suitable wood could be obtained. While bacon was frying, Mc-Cue mixed up a batch of baking powder biscuits and popped them into the oven. The coffee pot was bubbling and sending out an appetizing aroma. White had gone over to the store and come back with a couple cans of corned beef and a can of peaches. The beef was for lunch the day we crossed the pass he explained. The peaches we ate with our hot biscuits and bacon.

"Tomorrow, boys," said McCue, "we'll try to make Sheep Camp. It is at the head of this canyon and the end of timberline. It's twelve miles and a hard pull too, but they tell me at the post here that it is still possible to use our sleds so that will beat packing."

I do not think any of us slept very well that first night. I know I did not. The bed was warm and comfortable enough with the heat reflected from our generous fire, but I lay there watching the sparks fly up through the treetops, and my thoughts ran backward to the family in the far-off Wisconsin, wondering what they thought when they had received my letter, and then I would look forward into the unknown future with all the glamour and uncertainties and wonder where I would be a year hence. The old-timers were off in slumberland first. In fact, George White gave quite audible notice of that fact. I think I was the last one to go to sleep, then all too soon I heard McCue raking the embers of last night's fire together.

"Come, come boys!" he admonished. "We will never make Sheep Camp at this rate!"

McCue in fact was our alarm clock from this time on. He seemed tireless and always up by daylight and had breakfast well under way before the rest of us had the sleep rubbed out of our eyes. I remember that for breakfast that morning we had pancakes and cocoa with a can of syrup from the post. McCue explained that would be the last syrup we would see for many a day, as it would be too heavy to pack.

After breakfast the sleds were loaded and well lashed and we struck out on the upward trail. With two men pulling and one pushing, a load of 400 pounds was easy when the going was at all good. However, it was a steady upward climb, in some places quite steep. At intervals the trail crossed and recrossed the river on more or less unstable ice bridges. We could see that the season was advancing fast and in a few days both snow and ice on the lower portions of the river would be gone.

By mid afternoon we were out of the canyon and came out on a basin-like expanse that led up over several steep inclines to the foot of the pass two miles away. Here in the finger of willows was an encampment of fifty or more men waiting an opportune day for a spurt over the summit. (This was Sheep Camp, so named according to uncertain records because many years previously a party of hunters had driven a flock of sheep or goats through and camped on the site.) We pitched our camp in as favorable a spot as we could find, but green willows make a poor fire at best and I am afraid that Alex rather lost his temper in trying to coax a baking fire out of them. One of the campers lounged over to our fire to pass the time with us. He and McCue were old acquaintances, and Hank Somers was introduced to us.

"Better get your stuff up as far as The Scales, George," Hank advised. "Then you will be ready to make a run if this blasted blizzard ever lets up. We've been here a week."

"We will do so tomorrow," replied McCue.

The morning was clear and a circle of peaks sparkled and glistened in the clear sunlight. All eyes were turned toward the pass but a cloud of snow-white vapor was rolling through it and curling down the mountainside toward our camp.

"Another day here in camp," growled Hank.

"Him blow lak hell!" said Tony Pewcult.

Well, we would be busy anyway getting our stuff up to The Scales a mile and half above us. In fact, we found we had to cut our loads in two, for the three pitches between us and The Scales were really immense hills, both long and steep. The Scales were simply a mass of huge boulders that had rolled down the mountain slopes. Some enterprising prospector had swung a balance pole between two of the boulders and with a weight (usually a sack of flour) on one end, the various items of the outfit were balanced so as to complete the weight for packing purposes. When our first load was delivered at The Scales, a boyish idea to coast down the incline to camp suggested itself to me.

"Let's coast clear into camp!" I exclaimed.

"More probably break your neck," said Alex.

As none of the others favored the idea, I determined to try it alone. I took it stomach down. The sled started off smoothly on a gradual slope, then came the first pitch where the speed accelerated rapidly. Then came another medium slope where I spun along at railway speed. The second and steepest pitch had several wavelike snow curls or drifts and here the sled, now going at terrific speed, took leaps of fifteen or twenty feet. The breath was almost knocked out of my body, but I hung on desperately with both hands clutching the side of the sled and my toes striking the snow from time to time on either side of the sled. The last half mile checked the speed so I rolled off at our camp breathless but whole. It was a thrilling ride but hardly one to be repeated! Another load that day put everything at The Scales except our camp and bare necessities.

Off to the left and a little above our camp was the outlet of a glacier that pushed out its front and dropped huge cakes of ice as big as meeting houses to fall a thousand feet into the valley. Several such masses had come crashing down during the day. I might note here that these scales were the scene of a destructive avalanche two or three years later, when sixty or seventy people lost their lives right where we were camped.

McCue had seen some Indians and made arrangements for them to pack our outfit to the summit as soon as it cleared. Early next morning Old One Eye looked in on us and said laconically, "Good day, go quick."

The pass was clear. All the camp was astir. We hastily swallowed our breakfast, packed our tarp and stove on our sleds, and made our way to The Scales, followed by One Eye and his crowd. The old Indian made up the packs at The Scales. One hundred pounds was a load for a man, and fifty pounds for a woman. A fifty pound sack of flour was hung on one end of the balance pole and enough outfit to equal it on the other end. Someone had marked the pole with notches so the distance of the weight and outfit from the center was equal. While we were getting the packages ready for the weighing, I noticed Old One Eye slyly moving the sack of flour out several notches beyond its proper notch. As a matter of fact, it took about sixty pounds of outfit to bring the balance to a level, but I made no comment on the action which was that much to our benefit, but which Old One Eye evidently thought was to his! All packs made up, we joined the procession now moving steadily toward the summit.

The climb to the summit was half or three quarters of a mile. The strong winds from the interior had packed a sheet of snow, hard as ice from top to bottom, covering rocks and precipices in one long, smooth slide. Previous climbers had cut steps the whole distance from bottom to top. The incline was as steep as a ladder against a building and a misstep would send a person with his pack to the bottom of the slope. In fact, one unlucky packer had that morning lost his balance when nearing the top and came whizzing down, unhurt in body but much ruffled in disposition, to make the climb again. So smooth was the slope and so clean the descent on the other side that the Indian packers simply sat down on their overalls that they had used for a pack strap and slid from top to bottom, the blue of the overalls painting a blue streak on the mountainside. Keeping step one behind the other, we made the summit about noon. The packers were paid off and we ate a hasty lunch.

"Hurry, big wind come quick" advised One Eye.

Fifteen minutes brought us to the jumping off place on the other side. There we realized the reason for One Eye's warning. Rolling up the slope, from the interior, was a dense cloud of vapor. It was within 1,000 feet of us as we gazed down upon it. The bottom of the slope was invisible. It ended in Crater Lake, McCue explained.

"Three of us get on this sled and down we go!" cried McCue. "Give us two minutes to get out of the way, then follow."

McCue, White, and Bob sat astride and dropped ~ literally just that! Down, down, and they disappeared in gloom.

"You bring the other sled, Fred," shouted Alex and he dashed down the slope followed by Ralph before I could utter a word of objection. The cloud was now within 500 feet of me and rapidly rising. What to do? I had not heard a sound from any of the others. It was now or never. So, mustering up all my will-power, I head the sled straight down the slope, drew a long breath and dropped. The cloud flew up to meet me, wrapped me in its cold embrace, almost smothered me with its icy breath. One minute, two minutes of gasping expectancy and I dashed out into clear air and onto the ice of Crater Lake where the others were awaiting me. (Editor's note: He had conquered Chilkoot Pass!)

"What was the matter? Why were you so long?" My partners chided me.

Chapter 4
The Chain of Lakes

Crater Lake, a circular body a mile in diameter, was at this time of the year covered with ice and snow. Its shores were a mass of igneous rocks and boulders. There were no trees or wood of any kind.

"Twelve miles to timber," stated McCue. "A long, hard tramp and no time to spare if we want to make camp before night."

A rocky, tortuous canyon led down from Crater Lake. The trail followed its course in a general way although we were compelled many times to climb over steep, rocky noses that obstructed the way. It was late in the afternoon when we entered the belt of timber and came to a bustling camp of one hundred or more men who had preceded us. The encampment was by an ice lake. Lake Lindeman is the first of a chain of beautiful lakes that stretch away for hundreds of miles in the direction we were to follow. The waters draining from these lakes form the Lewes River, one of the main tributaries of the Yukon River.

We lost no time in pitching camp and getting a warm meal. We had had a hurried breakfast and only a cold bite on the summit, so we were ready for a good supper. By this time we had systematized our procedure when making camp and a word of explanation just here may be interesting. Bob White, who hailed from Maine, and his uncle George White were expert ax men, like all New England pioneers, and their part of the evening work was to provide the material for a fire. Two or three large green logs, ten or twelve feet long, were piled one on top of another for backlogs. These were usually held up by leaning against two convenient trees eight or ten feet apart. Two more green logs placed in front of these backlogs and only separated for a few inches, were supported on two green blocks or convenient stones. Under these last logs a fire of dry wood was laid and it was then ready for the cooks. On these slightly separated andirons our spiders, coffeepot, and kettles and pails rested while the meals were cooking. Alex and I usually acted as cooks in the evening. A pot of beans was kept simmering at one end of the ten-foot range. The coffee pot would be at the other end, a spider of bacon or fresh meat would be cooking near the center, and still other utensils would come in play to make our warm bannocks or pancakes.

Yukon River.

McCue had showed us a scheme for bannocks that we liked very much. Flour, baking powder and a pinch of salt were mixed, then just enough water added that the mass could be worked into a stiff dough. It was shaped into a flat cake about an inch thick and the size of one of our frying pans. Placed in a pan over the fire for a few minutes, we slightly browned it on one side, then with a quick flip of the hand turned it upside down and it was then browned on the other side. It was now stiff enough to be set up edgewise before the fire, leaning against a rock that had been heating. Half a dozen of these bannocks were prepared each evening, usually some being left over for breakfast. They had a flavor entirely different from the hot biscuits we baked in the Yukon stove. This latter was usually called into play at the noon hour when we did not stop long enough to prepare the elaborate fire we had at night.

While the fire makers and cooks were busy, McCue and Ralph saw to the beds. The tarpaulin was stretched up, the opening facing the fire and about six feet back from it. A generous floor of spruce boughs covered the ground, or rather the snow. This latter was either scraped away or trampled flat. In fact, we rather preferred leaving the snow as it did away with any irregularities in the ground, and with a foot or more of springy flat spruce boughs, there was no moisture from melting snow. Sometimes a convenient log was placed for a seat, but more often we simply sat back on the edge of the bed and ate our supper holding our plates in our laps.

How we did enjoy those evening repasts! After a hard day's tramp to lie back on the boughs and bask in the warmth of the fire, listen to the tales McCue and the older White were spinning while smoking their pipes, and to see the gleam of the flames reflected in the dark spruce woods was the height of luxury. With the fire replenished, the "andirons" supplemented with several other logs piled against the backlogs, we were insured an all night's heat and ample coals for morning.

On the morning of our first camp at Lake Lindeman while McCue was getting breakfast, I heard a peculiar noise. "Rrrr-ip-whish-rrr-ip-whish" it went.

"What in the world is that sound?" I asked, starting up.

"What? Oh that's a couple of men whipsawing," explained McCue.

"Whipsawing?" I questioned, "what for?"

"Oh, getting out lumber for their boat," he replied.

By this time the other boys were up and breakfast was ready. While we ate McCue explained more about the situation to us.

"You know, there is a chain of lakes here, one feeding into the other and lastly into the Yukon River. Now we can stop here, build our boats and when the ice goes out nothing to do but float down by water all the way to Forty Mile. That is what these men propose to do. If we had a heavy outfit I would be in favor of doing the same thing, but we are light and if we push on across the whole chain of lakes and build our boats below the last one, we will gain several weeks or a month over these fellows. The days are getting long and the traveling will be pleasant. What do you boys say about it?"

Before we could reply he continued, "Another thing, after the ice goes out on these lakes there is most always a head wind blowing up the lakes and at Windy Arm and Lake Laberge, which is forty miles long, I have known parties to be wind-bound for more than a week."

His advice to push on across the chain of frozen lakes, under the circumstances, certainly seemed good and we voted unanimously to follow it. It was the middle of April now. The sun was fast climbing northward. We could notice each day lengthening. The mornings were crisp and cold but by noon the snow on the trails was softening. The moccasins which we wore in the forenoon were changed to rubber boots at noon. We noticed a great difference in the traveling. In the morning, with a crisp, crackling snow underfoot and in our light, flexible moccasins it was a pleasure to step into the cold, clear air.

We would start right out at a brisk, invigorating pace, and we made good time, singing or whistling a song, but afternoons in our heavy boots and on a soft, mushy snow the trail grew heavy. We finally adopted the plan of a very early start and pushed on until the snow softened too much, then would camp over until next morning. Even in this way we averaged twenty miles a day.

On starting out before crossing Lake Lindeman, McCue had advised us to adopt the Indian method of preventing snow-blindness, a most painful affliction. We blackened our eyebrows and our cheeks just below the eyes with charcoal and tucked several springs of green spruce twigs under our caps so the spray hung over our eyes. In this way none of us was affected by the glare of the snow, but we passed several camps where the occupants were laid up, sometimes for as much as two weeks, helpless and in great pain from the affliction.

One day followed another. We arrived at Lake Bennett, a still larger lake later to be the head of steamboat navigation and where a town of thousands of inhabitants grew with the Dawson rush a little later on. From Bennett we went to Windy Arm, which was well named, being a large lake with an arm coming in from the south connecting with Lake Atlin. Beyond Windy Arm lay Taglish Lake and Lake Marsh. A stream of considerable size fed from one lake to another. Our trail followed the surface of the stream. This was generally icebound and safe, though where a canyon occurred with swift, turbulent water, the going was precarious. Sometimes it was over a mere shelf of ice along a rocky bluff, then over an ice bridge to the other side (more or less unsafe), and once in a while there would be a stretch of open water where we had to take to the bluffs and lift and haul our sleds over the rocks until we could lower them to safe ice below.

Chapter 5

A Chilling Raft Ride

A river connecting the last two of the lakes seemed to be all open water and McCue advised building a raft. This we did of dry spruce logs. The sleds with well-lashed loads and themselves lashed to the raft occupied the center of the craft. With poles and improvised oars we pushed out into the swift stream and began the rather dangerous trip. I remember I had shot a couple of geese that morning and I spent my time plucking them and getting them ready for dinner. I planned to boil them and have dumplings with the stew, a dish I had prepared once before and which was highly praised by my companions. Anyone who has plucked the feathers and down from a goose will know what a job it was. Finally, the two were finished, cut up and in a large kettle ready for cooking. Up to this time I had scarcely noticed our progress, but several excited exclamations from Alex, who was at the head of the raft, now caught my attention. We were rapidly drifting down a narrow, high-walled canyon, and the bed of the stream was dotted with large boulders. Alex was giving directions so as to shift the unwieldy raft from side to side to avoid striking any of the dangerous obstructions.

"Hard over to the left!" shouted Alex just as the geese were finished.

But it was too late! A sunken rock just below the surface of the water caught the front of the raft and the momentum and the push of the current behind shoved the raft high up on the rock, where it hung for a moment, then the current caught the rear end and the raft simply jackknifed and spilled all of us and every loose article into the water. I came up gasping from the icy plunge and struck out for the shore, fortunately only a short distance away. Ralph was floundering near me and I pulled him ashore. George White and Bob followed. Alex, who was on the bow of the raft, was clinging to the end of it high above the water line, and McCue, who had the steering oar, had caught a line and climbed up onto the loaded sleds, which while now under water were still safely lashed to the raft. What to do and how to get the raft away?

From the Arc
of the
Circle District
Historical Society
Central, Alaska

Shooting Whitehorse Rapids, Yukon River.

McCue managed to get a line loose which Alex fastened to the nose of the raft. This he threw to the four of us on the shore. We had to wade out into the icy water up to our waists to catch it, but after a couple of throws we secured it. With the four of us pulling and McCue pushing with a pole, we managed to slide the raft off its anchorage and it righted itself and floated free below the dangerous boulder. There was no chance to camp there. There was no wood, either. We were wet, cold, and by this time, hungry. We could do nothing but get aboard and float on to where we could camp and overhaul our water-soaked possessions. That was a chilly ride. Five miles more of swift water passed under us before the canyon opened on a sandy flat with wood in abundance. The remainder of that day and all the next were spent in drying our bedding and provisions. But where were my geese? Alas! Both geese and bucket were on the bottom of the river! Our sugar and salt had dissolved. Coffee in a can was safe. The flour was only wet in half an inch on the sacks and the bacon, of course, only needed drying. Our blankets and clothing were hung upon lines to dry. A rousing fire and our exertions dried the clothes on our bodies. That night we had our coffee without sugar. Bald-headed coffee Ralph called it.

"But it might have been worse," commented McCue, and so we all felt.

When we were dried out, we again took to the raft until we came to solid ice once more where it was abandoned for the sleds. We were approaching Miles Canyon, the scene of so many fatalities a few years later when the Klondike Rush was on. The river cuts for three-fourths of a mile through a basalt dyke, its perpendicular walls only a hundred or two feet apart. The terrific speed of the water, and the tremendous swells, render running a boat through a feat for only the most experienced boatmen. In the center of the canyon is a notch in one of the side walls which causes a whirlpool where a floating object is carried around and around until it is finally sucked down to disappear. A whole tree will be drawn into its mane to be at last shot out of the mouth of the canyon stripped of all its branches and even denuded of its bark. Our trail led us over the bluff and around this deadly menace, and we all felt thankful to McCue that we had not stopped to build our boats on the lakes above only to have to face this monster later on. Five miles below the canyon was Whitehorse Rapids where many other fatal accidents occurred. Here was to be located the town of Whitehorse, later the terminal of the White Pass and Yukon Railroad.

"One more lake, but the largest of all," announced McCue, "Lake Laberge, forty miles long."

We had an unexpected surprise at this lake. Instead of being snow-covered, the ice was clear and smooth. It was a glorious sight.

"Oh for some skates," signed Alex.

"We can beat that," replied McCue. "Instead of a head wind it will be at our backs here and we will put up our tarps and make the wind push us."

A mast was rigged up, the two sleds hitched together and we pushed off. One man held the gee pole of the first sled and partly sliding, partly running he kept us headed in the right direction. As the wind increased we gathered speed and by suppertime we had accomplished the whole forty miles and were camped on the far shore of the last lake. We now had a broad, stately stream before us that wound in majestic curves through quite a basin-like valley.

"Looks like good farming land," commented Alex.

April had now passed into the first of May. It was now four weeks since we had crossed the summit. On the evening of the first of May, Saturday, we camped on an island near the mouth of a large stream coming in from the south. It was the Hootalinqua announced McCue. I had noticed McCue

31

examining the timber along the banks of the stream as we passed.

"Good timber on this island," he stated, "guess we will build our boats here. We'd better make a good camp as we'll likely be here a week or more."

We were far ahead of any other men that year. The last camp we had seen was at Whitehorse. There was a foot of snow under the trees. This we cleared away around our camp down to a carpet of moss. The tarpaulin was stretched and a good bed provided of spruce boughs. More than usual pains were taken with the fireplace and arrangements for cooking. The morrow was the Sabbath.

"We'll take a day of rest," announced McCue. "Then Monday morning we'll begin our boats."

Two men whipsawing lumber.

Chapter 6
Waiting for the Ice to Break

Our camp was on one of the islands that from here on were numerous throughout the course of the Yukon. The island was heavily wooded with the spruce which from now on was to be the prevailing tree of the interior. Seldom reaching two feet in diameter, it grew to a height of seventy or eighty feet. It had a rather soft white wood. The tree had the peculiarity of retaining its small, globular cones for years, until sometimes the mass must have weighed hundreds of pounds. Filled with pitch, these tops made a terrific, hot fire. Scattered among the spruces were several of the white paper birches, so common in the East and New England states. Remembering that the birch used to run sap when tapped as freely as the sugar maple, I tried several trees that day, but with no results. Their veins were still sealed in old winter's grasp.

A broad sheet of ice stretched away off to the southward where the Hootalinqua emerged and the stream we had been following likewise was icebound. It did not look as if the boats McCue proposed to build would be needed for months yet. But Monday morning saw us up bright and early. Breakfast was soon over and McCue took charge of operations.

"First a sawpit," he ordered.

Four convenient trees that formed a rectangle were cut off about six feet from the ground. On these, two timbers forty feet long were placed and securely fastened. These timbers were parallel and about eight feet apart. Two six-inch skids were placed across these sides and the "pit" was ready.

"I don't see why it is called a sawpit." I questioned.

"Well," said McCue, "in the old country where they used to get out lumber in this way there was an actual pit where the underman stood so they did not have to put up a frame, as we have, but in this country with its frozen soil that is not practical, so we build our pit above ground. It works just as well and you will work just as hard. Now for our logs. Here, Bob, down with this tree. Cut off a 36-foot log."

Bob jumped to his task and in a few minutes down crashed the spruce. The requisite length was cut off and all hands turned in to haul and roll the log to the side of the pit where two skids had been placed. With a rolling hitch such as lumbermen understand, the log was soon in place on the pit frame. The ax men had scored the bark along the sides of the log so a chalk line to guide the sawyers could be snapped.

"There now," directed McCue, "you, Fred, and you, Alex, ought to make good sawyers. You go on top, Fred, you are the lightest. Here is your saw. You have a line on top and Alex has a line directly underneath. If each of you holds your saw to your line you will do a smooth job."

The heavy seven-foot saw was passed up and I grasped my set of handles and Alex his handles attached to the lower end.

"Now," advised McCue, "easy does it. Just let the teeth in lightly, Fred, so it won't jerk and catch. Give a kind of rolling motion to it. You'll soon catch on and it will cut like butter."

That was good advice but hard to follow. Standing on the round surface of a twelve inch log and raising that heavy saw as far above my head as my arm could reach, then giving it the light, rolling downward swing so the teeth just bit into the wood without catching hold too severely required practice! I remember that the first hour was a series of jerks and stops. Once I came down with a severe bump on the handles. How my back and arms ached with the unusual strain, but occasionally the clear cutting "rrrr-ip" sang out on the air of a successful feed. These boards were only one half inch thick and about six inches wide.

While Alex and I were busy with our part of the work, the rest of the crew had not been idle. A framework for the boat was constructed, ribs ripped out of the slabs we had first cut off from the sides of our timber. A prow was fashioned and the bottom board of the boat laid. White was busy using the plane, smoothing the long, slim boards and beveling one edge so as to make a lap joint.

In three days one boat was completed. It was thirty-two feet long, had a five-foot beam, was sharp and very pointed at one end and only slightly less so at the other. The seams had been well caulked with pitch we had brought with us. Oars and oar pins and a strong paddle completed the work.

"There," said McCue with satisfaction, "that boat will ride any water on the Yukon and will make a dandy poling boat for the Forty Mile."

In three more days the other boat was also completed, a perfect twin of the first. It was Saturday night again, and our guide, McCue, announced that Sunday would be a day of rest again, then we would be off for Forty Mile. We had been on the island a week, but what a week! Besides the new and interesting work we had accomplished with our hands, stupendous changes had been taking place, changes which annually usher in the coming of spring to the Northland. On Wednesday we had noticed a notable rising of the ice in the river. Sharp, reverberating cracking detonations announced the breaking loose of the ice along the shores, but no forward movement of the ice could be detected. All day Thursday and Friday the ice gradually rose. It was creeping higher and higher up the banks. McCue was evidently worried.

"If the Hootalinqua breaks before this ice moves, it may pile up here on the island and flood us out," he explained.

Saturday morning just as we were completing the second boat we heard a crashing, booming sound from far up the river.

"She's breaking!" McCue shouted. Then catching sight of the Yukon ice which had begun slowly moving downstream like a gigantic ice snake, he continued, "Glory be! Our ice goes too; so unless she jams just below us, we're safe!"

That was a tremendous exhibit of power to witness. Crashing, roaring, tumbling down came a mass of ice water and broken trees. Twenty, thirty, forty feet it reared its head. It was sweeping everything before it. Would it halt when it reached the Yukon or would it rush on and go plowing across our island and sweep us and our camp into eternity? We held our breath. With a crash, the Hootalinqua flung its gorge into the Yukon and plowed halfway across the stream, but the mightier mass of the mother river prevailed and the onward rush was turned down and joined to the larger flow.

"All is right now, boys," ejaculated McCue triumphantly, "by Monday the ice will be out and we can start."

But the breakup of the ice was not the only change I noticed. Where we had shoveled away a foot of snow the previous week for our camp, flowers were now blooming. Those dormant birch trees that would not yield a drop of sap now had swelling buds and even leaves as large as a mouse's ear. Winter had gone and spring had almost leaped into summer in one short week! Yes, before we reached Forty Mile a week later, we found wild roses blooming along the banks where still great masses of ice lay melting like grisly ghosts of winter in the lap of summer. Soon the ground was to be carpeted with moss a foot thick and amid its green masses I would gather handfuls of wild cranberries, remains of last summer's product. On the mountainsides were old-fashioned wind flowers, or anemones, and yellow buttercups.

Chapter 7

The Yukon Voyage

Stampeders

On Monday morning with all our outfit safely stowed in the two boats, we launched them on the rushing flow and were whirled away on our north-bound course. How easy it was after our month of arduous sled work, to sit back in the boat and watch the shores glide swiftly by, our only exertion an occasional dip of the paddles to keep the boat in the main current and away from the sweepers, the overhanging trees that had been partially undermined by the raging torrent.

On the heads of the islands were piled up masses of ice and driftwood and whenever the river closed into canyon-like conditions the ice had been shoved up on the banks in great masses, twenty feet high in places. These ice walls were continually breaking down and falling into the river so that a watchful eye was needed to prevent getting caught under a fall, or swamped by the huge wave sent rushing out into the stream.

McCue had told us about two bad spots of water we would encounter sometime that afternoon. Five Fingers and then five miles below that, Rink Rapids.

Toward three o'clock we noticed McCue's boat pulling into the shore and Mc-Cue himself waving us to do the same.

"The Five Fingers are just below us, boys," he warned. "Let's take a look at them and see what they are like."

A quarter of a mile below us a basalt dyke crossed the river. Three huge masses rose sheer up and out of the water, dividing the current into three channels. These three rocks with the two on either bank had given the name of Five Fingers to the location. We mounted the bluff high above the scene and looked down upon it. The water confined into the three narrow channels roared through like a millrace. The noise was deafening. Just under our feet was an enormous gorge full of seething whirlpools. This was the right-hand channel, much the largest of all, but in McCue's estimation the safest as the chute was nearly straight whereas the other two made a sharp turn just as the rocks were passed. The current in the center of the chute was arched and fully three feet higher than on the rocky sides. At the lower end of the chute the water rose in three enormous swells, each with a curling, breaking tip of white water.

"It's all right, boys," yelled McCue above the river's roar, "if you follow directions and don't lose your heads! Now, you see that swell in the center? Head your boat straight for that and keep on it. Don't let your boat swing sideways and strike the wall. It would go to pieces like a matchbox. If you hit those swells head-on, the boat will ride them like a duck. Now follow us and watch sharp,"

I knelt in the bow with a paddle. Ralph sat in the center of the boat manning the oars and Alex had the stern. Ralph and I were to row and paddle for all we were worth, so as to keep the boat moving faster than the water, giving Alex a chance to steer. Slowly we swung out into midstream, a hundred feet behind the lead boat. We saw it drawn toward the opening, rapidly increasing in speed, then dip over the brow and disappear. Our boat was not far behind. Just as we made the first plunge I caught a glimpse of the other boat as it rose on the crest at the first swell, then our own needs took all our attention. Frantically I used the paddle first on one side then on the other. Ralph was doing the best he could, but the boiling water tore and wrenched at his oars so, as he later confessed, he did more harm than good. However, Alex and I held the boat on the crest through the chute and we struck the first wave head-on squarely. A sheet of water and spray drenched us, but the boat rose through it and seemed pointing to the sky as we emerged, then it made a downward plunge and we struck the second and largest swell. Our luck was still with us and we made that successfully as we did the third and last. When we emerged into the basin below, the other boys were awaiting us. They too had made the passage with nothing worse than a drenching. Landing, we bailed out the few buckets of water we had shipped, then were off again.

Five miles below us were the Rink Rapids. Another basalt dyke broke the current, but the swells were no worse than those we had just traversed, so we made the passage without difficulty. From here on the river rapidly grew larger from the accession of the numerous tributaries. Little and Big Salmon Rivers from the south joined at a point where we found some Indian villages. The Pelly River, the largest of all the tributaries, the White River with its milky current from the glaciers at its head, the Stewart River from the Rockies to the east, then the Klondike which a few years later was to be the scene of the great gold rush, and lastly the Forty Mile all fed into the Yukon. As the river enlarged, its valleys widened, and in many places were miles in width. These valleys were some day to be the scene of great agricultural activities, but now we saw but three white men in the five hundred miles we ran with our boats. One was George Carmack, who lived with his two Indian women at a small trading post on the Lewes River, and on an island near to the mouth of the Pelly were Joe Ladue and A. Harper who ran a trading post there.

Their trading post was one of the three established by the Alaska Commercial Company when it took over the territory of the Russian Fur Company at the time of the purchase of Alaska in 1867. There was quite a romance attached to the founding of these posts. Harper, Jack McQuesten, and Al Mayo were three young men who had entered into the employ of the Hudson's Bay Company. They had been located far to the north on the McKenzie River. Conditions were so unsatisfactory to them that they had escaped from the dominion of the Hudson's Bay Company and crossed the range of the Rocky Mountains to the head of the Porcupine River. There they got an Indian canoe, and had just followed the Porcupine to the Yukon, then on down the Yukon to the Bering Sea, hoping to catch up with a whaler and so make their way back to the United States. At St. Michael they met the officials of the Alaska Commercial Company and were persuaded to go back up the Yukon and establish trading posts for that company. Harper located near the Pelly River, McQuesten at Forty Mile, and Mayo near the mouth of the Tanana River. All three of these men had a great deal to do with the development of the interior of Alaska. At first they had only Indians for traders and dealt in furs. They took Indian wives. With the influx of miners, their businesses rapidly expanded and many an old sourdough like myself had grateful memories of the help he received from their hands in years of bitter need.

Chapter 8
Forty Mile and Fort Cudahay
Summer, 1894

Circle Hot Springs.

It was five hundred miles to Forty Mile, our summer destination, which we reached on the first of June. Forty-two days had been required to accomplish the eight hundred miles from Juneau. Forty Mile was the supply point of the largest mining camp on the Yukon. It was a rambling village of a score or two of log cabins with one a little larger than the others. The former were the winter homes of the miners now back in the gulches at their summer work. The larger building was the store of McQuesten. Here, once a year, came supplies brought to St. Michael at the mouth of the Yukon by ocean steamers from San Francisco, then up the Yukon by the riverboat *Arctic*. Leaving the mouth of the river as soon as the ice went out, she was due at Forty Mile thirty days later with her yearly supplies. Her arrival was the greatest annual event. All the miners came in from their claims, Indians in their canoes dropped down from their homes on the various streams, even the newcomers, chachawkas, like ourselves, caught the excitement. For with the arrival of the *Arctic* came fresh supplies, letters, newspapers, books, and mail. What difference did it make that the papers and letters were a year old, having lain at St. Michael over the winter months? They were still the latest news and no less welcome.

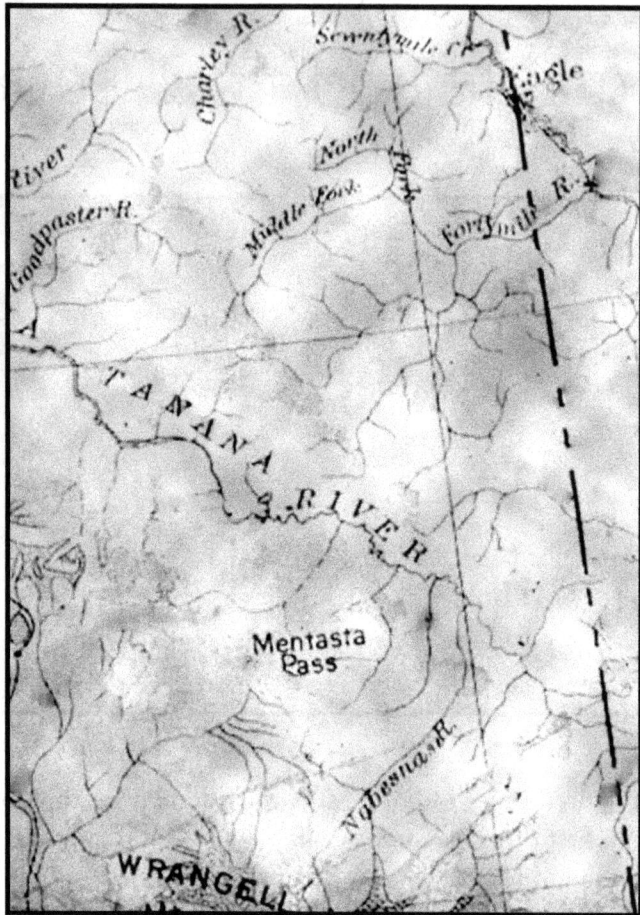

Forty Mile Country.

A generous reward was always offered by McQuesten to the Indian who first caught sight of the *Arctic* with her single smokestack as she came into sight around the bend near a creek seven miles below the post. With the cry of "Steamboat, steamboat!" pandemonium would break loose. Hundreds of rounds of ammunition were fired, the dogs howled in sympathy, and the *Arctic* would respond with her steam whistle which echoed off the hills. An hour later, after the boat had tied up at the bank, a mob of willing hands would rush to help with the unloading. Sacks of flour, beans, and bacon would be piled in the warehouse, canned goods in limited quantity came next, then would be sugar. "Fifty pounds for everybody!" the mate would yell. Then, of course, there was tobacco, and whiskey galore. There were no vegetables or fruit. Mining tools, clothing, hardware would complete the load. The night after the arrival of the steamboat was a night of wild carousal and drinking. Prospectors had come in from many creeks and their tales of new strikes would cause a stampede the next day. The more clear-headed and sober men at once sought the trading post and bought their year's supplies of provisions and had them carried to their cabins and safely stored there.

The old-timers still tell of the year, a few years prior to our arrival, when they looked in vain for the *Arctic* with her load. Day after day and week after week passed and still the cry of "steamboat" did not resound. At last came an Indian paddling up in his canoe to tell of the sinking of the *Arctic* near the mouth of the river, one thousand miles below, with the loss of all her cargo! All that could do so immediately departed upstream in poling boats on the long and hazardous trip outside. The few who remained inside existed as best they could on the meager remaining provisions in the posts, supplemented with the game that could be killed. It was related by George Snow and his party of four that a single sack of flour was their sole stock of manufactured provisions. Mushrooms were gathered in the woods, rabbit and caribou furnished the rest of their living, but it was a long and dreary wait until the recovered *Arctic* came forging up the river a year later.

But better times were coming. The fall previous to our arrival, a new trading company, The North American Trading and Transportation Company, had arrived on the scene. This company, organized by the Captain John J. Healy who had had a trading post at Dyea, was financed by Cudahy International of Chicago and the Captain himself was on the scene ready and anxious to open a post. He had located a mile below Forty Mile on an elevated flat terrace just above a high bluff that turned the Yukon nearly at right angles to its former course. The location was ideal. Already work had commenced on the buildings of the post. We liked the atmosphere of the area. We dropped down with our boats to interview Captain Healy. His advice, while no doubt tinctured with his desire to obtain help, was no doubt very sound.

"It's this way, boys," he said. "You have no outfit in the first place to carry you through the summer at the mines up Forty Mile. If you start up now with your boats and outfit there would not be more than a month of working days left before the season closes. Besides, I am not sure you would find work now so late in the season. It's a long, hard, dangerous, very dangerous, trip up over the rapids too, but I don't suppose that would influence you! Now my advice is this: I will give you steady work all summer at $100 per month and board, and I will guarantee you the best outfit the post contains this fall. Besides, there are numerous parties out prospecting and if you are here at the post you will hear of it first and be in a position to make a run for the new diggings, or probably what is better, buy an interest in some of the claims and be glad to sell a share of your generous outfit to those hungry prospectors of the summer claims who are really in need of grubstake."

We talked Captain Healy's offer over and Alex, Ralph and I decided to accept it. McCue, of course, had his claim on Franklin Gulch and Bob and his uncle would go with him. So our pleasant party broke up and bidding goodby and good luck, to McCue and his partners, we went down to Fort Cudahy, as Captain Healy called his post, and started our summer's work.

We were soon joined by three other young men who for several years to follow were quite intimately associated with me. John Crist was a Wisconsin boy, although he had lately come from Montana where he had been working as a bridge carpenter for the Northern Pacific Railroad. Jim Bullard was from New York State and Sam "Kelley" Richards was from North Carolina. The two latter had been crew boys in Montana until lured by the tales of gold in Alaska. We six formed a corps of workers that the Captain depended on through the season. We ate at his table, and the Captain knew how to set a good table, too. A few weeks later his wife, and her maid, Olli, came in over the same trail we had followed, and about this time the boat-builders on Lake Lindeman and Bennett arrived, proving that McCue was right in stating we would beat them by several weeks.

That was an interesting summer. We first set up a sawmill and as soon as the logs began to arrive we started cutting them up. Captain Healy made arrangements with several gangs of the new men to go up the river and bring down logs in small rafts. Some of the Indians also would come in towing three or four logs. Everything was grist for the Captain. A sharp lookout was kept and whenever a raft was seen approaching, we manned a boat and rushed to help bring it to land, for unless guided close to the shore the swift current would carry it past the post, and once the raft got by it was lost, for the precipitous bluffs below the post and rapid current prevented any return. More than once we had exciting close calls and indeed several rafts were lost.

Alex, who claimed to have worked in a sawmill in Minnesota, was made sawyer and as soon as there was a supply of logs and lumber, Crist and I were set to putting up buildings. These were built much as were the cabins of the miners. Our logs were squared by the mill, but we notched the ends and each tier of logs was laid in a bed of moss that later was tamped into the cracks firmly. One of the buildings we put up had a large room that was designed for social purposes. A library of books and a billiard table were something quite new to the Yukon and caused some of the old sourdoughs to shake their heads in disapproval. A pack of cards and their tobacco and pipes had been sufficient for them.

So passed the summer very pleasantly. The days were long; sunshine and showers alternated. Sundays we did what washing and mending was necessary, and I spent many hours roaming the hills or investigating the nearby creek, collecting and pressing flowers that by this time of year grew in riotous profusion. Sometimes the Captain held our attention for hours with tales of early adventures in Montana and Idaho where he had been a fur-trader. He had had battles with Indians and narrow escapes. Healy was an Irishman with a hasty temper that sometimes made enemies for him, but like all his class, he was generous and faithful to a friend. I will always hold him and Mrs. Healy in grateful memory.

By the end of July, Indians and their dogs began to collect at Forty Mile and Cudahy. It was getting near steamboat time. The Indian dogs were a nuisance, I might say almost a menace. Never regularly fed by their owners, they had learned to steal, and being always half-starved, were really dangerous. Mrs. Healy had a large, fine looking, good-natured dog she called Crib. He was her bodyguard and when Mrs. Healy took a walk, Crib accompanied her. Hanging around the post seeming to belong to nobody, but very much at home, was a mongrel sort of cur that we had dubbed Ginx. For some reason we never could understand, Crib and Ginx were inseparable friends, but while Crib was the best natured dog in the post, Ginx was the most quarrelsome. It was his delight as soon as an Indian dog pack invaded the post to dash in and start a fight, calling on Crib for help. This Crib never failed to do, but as soon as the fight was well underway Ginx retired to the top of a lumber pile and apparently sat there to umpire the scrap. Poor Crib, fighting a whole pack of savage dogs, was always cut and scarred from his generous attempts to rescue his faithless pal. One day, however, the tables were turned. Crib had gone walking with Mrs. Healy and when Ginx started the usual

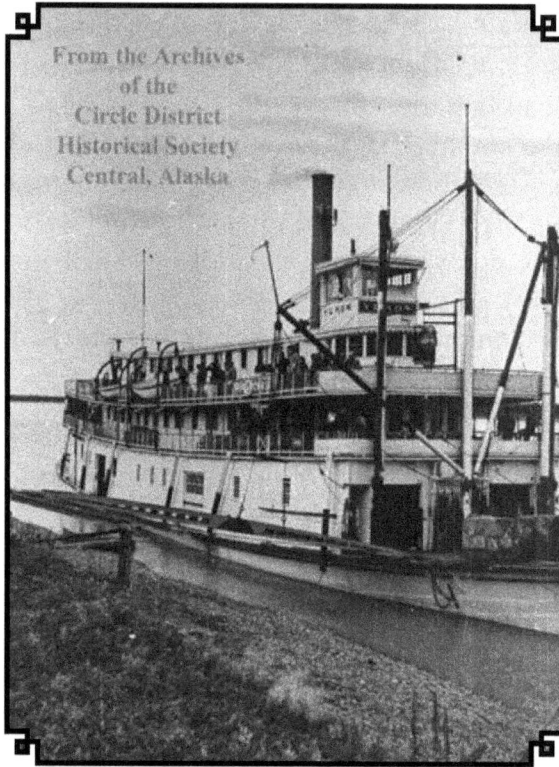

From the Archives
of the
Circle District
Historical Society
Central, Alaska

Yukon at Circle City.

fight and called for Crib to help him, Crib was not there, and the way that pack of Indian dogs mauled and bit and scared Ginx did our hearts good. I doubt if we would have lifted a hand to save him, but he finally broke away from the pack and crawled under a pile of lumber where for two days we could hear his whining and moaning before he crawled out a sadder and wiser dog.

With the approach of steamboat time, miners also began to come in from the gulches. Indians were posted on the heights below the post. Everyone was on the qui vive. Just as our noon whistle blew one day, we heard the faint call of "Steamboat, steamboat!" We rushed to the bank. Dinner was forgotten. Nothing was in sight, but away down the river came the sound of a powerful exhaust "whosh — whosh."

"That's the *Arctic*! I know her exhaust!" yelled Tom-the-Turk.

"Bet you an ounce it's the *P.B. Weare*," offered Hank Somers.

Other bets were quickly made and taken. Ten minutes later a smudge of smoke showed above the treetops and the *Weare* with her two smokestacks came into view. This was Captain Healy's supply boat.

"Well, the *Arctic* won't be far behind," said Tom, and as a matter of fact she did arrive the next day.

Both posts were soon well stocked with new outfits and Captain Healy announced that the *P.B. Weare* would return immediately to St. Michael and be back with a second load before the Yukon closed. Such a thing had never happened before on the river, and many a dubious head shake showed the doubt in the minds of the old-timers that it could be accomplished. The *Arctic* had never made but one trip a year, but the Captain was as good as his word and immediately his boat was unloaded it was started down the river. As a matter of fact, the boat did make the return trip successfully.

July passed into August, and August into September. The last of the miners had come in from their claims, for by now the days were shortening and ice forming in the sluice boxes prevented further work that year. True to his word, Captain Healy had set us aside a liberal outfit. Our personal party had now dwindled to four. Alex had gone down the river on the *P.B. Weare* and intended going outside. We never saw him again. Poor Ralph, tired of the sawmill, had drifted over to Forty Mile and was working in a saloon. I saw him years later in Nome, a mere bum, washing out spittoons and sweeping the floor for his meals and drinks.

Bullard, Kelly, Crist and I were a congenial quartet. We bought our outfit in common. I remember we had twelve sacks of flour, three of bacon, five hundred pounds of bacon, a barrel of sugar, one of oatmeal, one of rice, and one hundred twenty pounds of butter in a barrel of brine. Butter was an unheard of luxury in those days. It cost us $120, but that did not matter! We also had two cases of assorted canned goods and one case of the then-new dehydrated vegetables. Then, of course, there were numerous little things like spices, tools, clothing, tents etc. We did not know where we would need this generous layout, but were glad to be sure of it.

About the first of September, a party of prospectors who had been in the Birch Creek country two hundred miles north of Forty Mile returned with fabulous reports of riches they had struck. They had the evidence too with them. Jack Gregor and Pat Kinnaly had Discovery on Mastodon Creek and panned out a thousand dollars in a week! George Harmen and Chris Harrington located just below this discovery. Other men who were near had rushed in and the whole six miles of the creek had been staked. In addition, not only Mastodon, but Miller, Independence, and Mammoth Creeks were staked. The common usage of miners' laws then prevailing allowed a discoverer two claims of 500 feet each on his discovery creek, and any miner could stake his one claim on each creek, so a comparatively small party as this one had been could practically stake out all the claims on several creeks. Of course, to hold these claims they had to be worked, so much work each year. The hope of the prospector was to sell an interest in a part of his claims for some money and secure a partner who would help to work the claims. There was no lack of buyers after the rich showing made by Pat and Jack!

Our quartet bought one-fourth interest each in Number 39, Mastodon, a promising area, from Jack Frost. Here was a place to use our outfit, but to do so we must first get it there. It was two hundred miles down the river to Circle City, as the new post was to be called. We would need a boat, or rather a scow. We went to Captain Healy for advice.

"Boys," he said, "I need your help to the very last minute. The river will keep open until about October 10, maybe later. Help me out this month. I will give you all the lumber you need to make your scow. You can build it on Saturdays and Sundays. What do you say?"

"That's fine of you, Captain," I replied. "We'll do it," and we did.

Every spare moment was devoted to building our scow. As I remember, it was eighteen feet long, eight feet wide with three-foot sides. Strongly built and braced and well caulked, we had it done by October first.

The days were getting perceptively shorter and colder. Rim ice formed along the shore but as yet no sign of floating ice had appeared. Old-timers told us we could figure on a week after the first floating ice showed before the river closed. We expected it would take that long to reach Circle City. The fifth of October there was a cold north wind and that evening we saw small patches of floating ice drifting by.

"Time to be off," said Jim.

We all agreed and Captain Healy also concurred with his advice.

"We'll see you boys there next year," he said, "I will have a post there too."

Chapter 9

Our Scow Trip to Circle City

Circle Hot Springs - taken from hillside above springs.

By daylight we were rushing our outfit aboard the scow and we shoved off. Our outfit and ourselves loaded it down to within four inches of the top. It was a most unwieldy craft and, owing to the depth of water it drew, exceedingly unsafe.

"Pretty heavy," commented Kelley looking over the side, "hope we don't run into any bad water."

We had set up our stove on a plank in the center of the boat so we could get our meals and not stop running as long as daylight lasted. Everything worked well the first day. A few sluggish pans of fragile ice were floating with the current. These patches had formed on the bottom of the river, mainly on the shallower, gravelly places. When sufficiently buoyant, the mass arose to the surface bringing gravel and small rocks with it. The ice bodies now gradually hardened, slowly revolving with the current, the edges rubbed up and crumpled like pie crust so one easily understood how the name "pans" came to be given to the cakes of ice.

The early evening found us looking for a place to camp and this we found behind a point where the current was sheared away from the shore. That was a cold camp. Too late and too dark to fix up a good bed, we had to be content with a fire and, rolling our blankets near it, passed the hours of darkness. As our whole year's provisions were in the scow, we agreed to take turns standing guard each night, and lots being cast, Jim Bullard was the lucky, or unlucky, recipient of the short one. With many a bantering expression of commiserations, the rest of us went to sleep, cautioning Jim to call us at the first streaks of daylight.

It seemed to me that I had scarcely dropped asleep when I was awakened by Jim's rich, melodious voice proclaiming that, "Patsy A. Flanigan had a bull pup; and sure, t'was of elegant stock, sir!"

John Crist seized a boot and declaring that he "would kill that pup!" provoked a deep, hearty, "haw, haw, haw!" from Jim, but he assured us that it was daylight, and we had been asleep eight hours.

Beds were hurriedly rolled and stowed away on board, the towline was cast off and we resumed our journey. The ice patches were thicker but gave no special trouble.

The previous day Kelly had been unanimously elected cook, with the understanding that he should be relieved from standing guard nights, so as soon as we were underway, he set about fixing breakfast. Under Kelley's skillful, quick manipulations, bacon and beans were soon sending out appetizing odors, coffee was bubbling in the pot, and as soon as the hot baking powder biscuits were taken from the oven we were invited to "throw it into you!" which we proceeded to do in total disregard to all laws of health or hygiene. The crisp, outdoor air encouraged us to devour an amount of hot bread, slapjacks, bacon, beans, and strong coffee that would paralyze an Eastern dyspeptic, and we felt none the worse for it!

Rolling up in his robes after breakfast, Jim announced that he was going to sleep. Two of us stationed ourselves at the steering sweeps, one at either side, and a sharp lookout was kept for sunken rocks or shoal bars.

Along in the forenoon we had an exciting incident. Approaching an island we were in a quandary as to which of the two channels to take. However, we were not to choose as our craft, after hesitating a moment, turned into the one on the left.

"It looks all right," said Kelley. But half a mile down, with a grating crush, the scow pushed up on a shoal bar in midstream and stopped.

"Jump overboard everybody," shouted Crist, "and hold her. Don't let her swing sidewise or she'll fill with water."

We all piled into the icy water and seizing hold of the sides, held the boat head-on. Relieved of our weight, the craft slowly pushed on a few more feet and hung up again.

"Hang on, boys," cried Jim, "and I'll see where the deep water lies."

He waded around on both sides and in front of the scow. The water was shoal for some distance then deepened. Ahead for fifty feet there was but two feet of water, then it too deepened. We were on a submerged island! How to move our heavily laden craft was the problem. We surveyed the situation in dismay, wondering what to do. Occasional pans of ice came bumping the stern of the scow and we realized that our situation a day later in such a spot would inevitably mean disaster.

"Nothing to do but lighten the boat and shove her over the bar," announced Crist. "Get out the barrel of butter and stand it on end. The water can't hurt that."

We did so, then a board placed on the barrel gave us a platform where we stacked several sacks of flour and bacon.

"Now try that, it ought to have lightened her a great deal," I commented.

We all lifted and shoved and slowly the scow scraped along until it floated freely in the deeper water. While two of us held it, the others got the flour and butter aboard and were off again, wet to the waist in icy water. We couldn't afford the time to stop and build a fire to dry out, but managed to dig up some dry clothing from our dunnage bags in exchange for our sodden ones.

"We'll have to stop early enough tonight to get a good fire and dry out," remarked Kelley. This we did, and around a rousing fire hung our wet garments to dry. This night was more comfortable than the previous one as we had time to provide a bed of spruce boughs and had a good fire that lasted until daylight.

The next two days were without special incident. The ice pans were getting thicker and it became more and more difficult to work the scow into a safe place for the night, but we accomplished it without accident. The fifth day we passed Seventy Mile, which was just an Indian camp at the mouth of the Charley River and so named because it was about seventy miles above our destination at Circle City. We passed this place about four o'clock in the afternoon and probably drifted five or six miles before we tied up for the night. We had a good deal of difficulty getting into the shore and missed two or three desirable looking camping spots.

"Another day's run ends it," prophesied Crist. "We either make Circle City or get froze in. This ice can't run much longer, just notice how thick it is and how logy the current."

It certainly was hazardous looking as we gazed out across the river the next morning. The pans almost covered the surface of the water and a steady grinding and crunching accompanied them. They were moving very sluggishly.

"Had we better chance it?" queried Kelley. "We might lose everything if we get caught in a jam!"

We decided to chance it. The scow had to be chopped out of anchor ice that had formed around it in the night. Crist and I stood by with poles one on either side to veer off the encroaching pans. We passed several islands where already the ice was piling up in large masses. As these grew larger and extended farther out into the river on each side, they caused the whirling pans to close in on each side and our situation grew really perilous.

Once we swung down a channel beside an island, our boat not fifty feet from the bank. A couple of men sprang up from a fire and racing alongside of us told how their scow had been crushed the previous day, leaving them marooned. The only thing they had saved was a sack of flour and when they caught sight of us they were baking some of the wet dough rolled on a stick. We were perfectly helpless to give them any aid, but shouting encouragement to them and promising to send help, we were borne on past them.

"Boys," said Bullard, "it looks to me that if we don't get to shore we may be in their fix or worse."

The predicament of the shipwrecked men brought that grim warning and thought very forcibly to our minds and we agreed to land at the first favorable opportunity. That was not easy. Ahead, we could see the ice stream dividing, part swinging into the shallow water where the cakes were piling up in jams around which the troubled current foamed and boiled. Would we miss it and keep with the main pack? Every muscle was strained. The perspiration poured from our faces. The scow stopped, undecided for a moment, and then slowly followed the ice along the deep channel.

We breathed easier, but our relief was of short duration. Just ahead we saw a wild commotion of tossing ice cakes and rolling waters. We were upon the rapids! The boat caught the impetus of the current and began to move at a livelier ate. We were powerless to do more than keep her headed straight. An immense flow, half an acre in extent, that was farther out in the stream and moving at an increased speed, came whirling along diagonally toward us, and bid fair to crush us between itself and the anchor ice along the shore. We clinched our hands and set our teeth in dismay, but the huge cake shot in just ahead of us, sending the smaller pieces flying in a shower up the bank. Dropping into the smooth water behind our ghostly pilot, we followed in its wake through the remainder of the rapids and saw below us the head of the great flats of the Yukon. Here, the channel spreads out for several miles and many islands fill the course. On every hand were bars and shoals, and on which the ice was piling up in large masses. We gradually edged toward the left hand bank on which Circle City was located, and finally managed to cut our way to the shore.

We all agreed that further progress was impossible with the scow, so our provisions were carried up to safety on the bank. The next morning, indeed long before morning, we heard the crashing and splintering of the ice as it caught and jammed again and at last settled into the stillness and immovability for the winter.

What a sight met our eyes in the morning! Instead of a smooth glassy surface as I had been accustomed to see on an Eastern stream when frozen, here were great cakes upended in all positions. Great ridges of them, some twenty feet high, with occasionally a smooth place between ridges, stretched across the river.

"Gracious," said Kelley, "what if we had been out in that when it jammed!"

It was indeed fortunate we had landed when we did. Our outfit was safe even if it did mean some extra labor to get it to Circle City. We built a substantial cache ten feet high where we placed all our provisions. Then a tent was set up and Kelley agreed to remain and watch our outfit while Crist, Bullard and I went on to Circle City and located a cabin site. Kelley also agreed to break up the scow to save the lumber for use in the cabin we expected to build.

We took a light load of provisions and our bedding with us as well as tools for cabin-building. Two miles below where we had stopped, by following the bank of the river, we came to an Indian village. Here was Alexander and his Birch Creek tribe. They had a fairly good trail to the new post, which was only seven miles away.

We soon heard the ring of axes and entering a beautiful strand of spruce trees found two of our friends hard at work. Walter Watson and Jerry Heater had left a week ahead of us, so had their cabin just completed.

"Right in here, boys," shouted Jerry. "Finest place for a cabin in the world and near enough to the post too. Build right alongside of us and bunk with us while you're building. Where's Kelley?" he continued.

We soon related our experience and told why Kelley remained behind.

"Well, I am sure glad you got in," Jerry replied. "I was getting worried about you."

It was, as he said, an ideal spot. There were several acres in the area where the spruces grew tall and straight, seventy or eighty feet high and about a foot in diameter. Bullard at once seized an ax and before dark had dropped a dozen trees.

A week went by, a week of busy work. Our cabin was up and enclosed, chinked with moss and the roof covered with moss and dirt. "We will leave the floor and door and use the lumber from the scow when we get it here," said Crist.

Next we had to go back to Kelley and get our precious provisions. We had two sleds so we thought three or four trips would make it. Kelley was glad to see us. He had gotten the scow in pieces and the lumber piled neatly up ready to haul. Bullard offered to swap places with him and after that we took turns staying guard until everything was in. It took four trips until all was packed to our cabin area. It was about nine miles and rather rough going. With the lumber from the scow, the floor to the cabin was laid, the door hung, a table made and four bunks built against the walls. We were ready for housekeeping, and none too soon, either, for already the nights were getting cold, the mercury indicating twenty to thirty degrees below zero. The sun rose later and set earlier. The arctic winter was upon us.

Chapter 10

Circle City

Winter, 1894

A council was held among us and a course of procedure decided. One would get the wood and water for a week, then cook for a week, then have a fortnight off while the others took their turns.

"Now remember," said Crist, "if anyone finds fault with what is being done, he will have to take that one's place!"

Crist nearly got caught with his own rule, for one morning when Kelley was cooking and the pancakes got burned, he announced, "That Kelley can't boil water without burning it ~ but, I like it a little scorched!" he hastily corrected himself.

Up to the time we had completed our cabin we had been too busy to visit the post, though it was but half a mile off down the river. We now walked down to see what was there in the way of civilization, buildings, and activities and to call on friends.

There were about one hundred log cabins strung out in a straggling manner along the bank of the river. This was a steep, high cut affair with deep water all along it. This fact had caused the selection of the site so necessary for a steamboat landing. One large building, Tom O'Brien's saloon, was the social center of the place. We knew this was the first place we should visit, and in here we met numerous friends and acquaintances, heard the talk of newly discovered diggings and learned that the general opinion was to remain in Circle City until about March, then freight our outfits to the mines in time for the spring openings.

"Four or five months," sighed Jim, "with nothing to do! Oh, I'll go crazy!"

Jim was never so happy as when working and I never saw such a man. He did not know what it was to be tired. Always good-natured, he and Crist were the life of the camp. Never were four young fellows more agreeably suited for a winter's sojourn in the arctic than was our party. With a comfortable cabin, well sheltered in thick timber, wood and water in abundance at our hand, and with an ample store of provisions, our creature comforts were assured. Nearly of the same age, all hopeful and full of anticipations, each one willing to do his share of the work and contributing toward the general goodwill

and comfort of the home, we formed a camaraderie of good fellowship that was never marred by the least jar of discord or wrangling.

Our cabin soon became a social gathering place, and indeed we were seldom without visitors from the town. Jim had a violin and Kelley a banjo. Kelley was from the south and knew all the old darky songs and melodies, and Jim, hearing the tune, had no difficulty in accompanying Kelley on the violin. All the latest outside songs such as "After the Ball," "Two Little Girls in Blue," and "Golden Slippers" were at their fingertips. Then Jerry Heater with his violin and Walter Watson with his harmonica joined in, and they always had appreciative audiences. Nearly every evening a musical entertainment was held, lasting far into the wee small hours of the morning.

Other evenings were passed in social dances, held in some miner's cabin. Stoves, bunks, and tables were cleared out for the occasion. The native Indian women quickly learned the steps, and waltzes, polkas and quadrilles were announced by the master of ceremonies without pause or interruption.

Some astonishing combinations of the milliner's art were devised by the dusky belles in honor of these occasions. Their footwear might consist of elaborately wrought moose-skin moccasins, with artistic silk and bead work, or the more picturesque mucklucks of seal skin and undressed caribou. Sometimes their parkas were of the warm caribou skins with their immense hoods trimmed with long wolverine fur, or foxtails; sometimes they were made of salmon or other fish skins, and the "Princess" even blazed forth in one made from flour sacks with bright red and blue letters announcing, "Baker's Best. Put up Especially for the Yukon Trade."

The miners have a predilection for uncouth sobriquets and these were not confined to themselves alone but extended to their dusky partners. "Crazy Baker" might be seen whirling around with "Short and Dirty" while his cabin partner, "The Laughing Frenchman," was bowing to her seat "Sarah Bernhart." "Tom-the-Turk" offered his arm to "Old Tattoo," and "Pete-the-Pig" was snubbed by "Slapjack Molly" who preferred "Handshaker Bob" for a partner.

Many long hours were passed away in games of whist, poker, or cribbage, while those more intellectually inclined were not wholly denied the delights of literature. Among the population of three hundred men representing nearly every vocation in life -- miners, bankers, merchants, mechanics, schoolteachers, lawyers, farmers, doctors, young college graduates, and engineers -- quite a store of reading matter was unearthed, and a book exchange established, from which one could select a varied catalogue from Grant's Memoirs or Scott's Waverly to the latest yellow paper dime novel.

A certain proportion of the old-timers were never happy outside of the walls of a saloon, and their earnings and energy were wasted at the bar or faro table, until long before spring their resources were exhausted and they were so deep "in the hole" that all they could earn during the following season would scarcely put them on their feet again. The process would be repeated again and again until debauchery and excess sapped their vitality and they would no longer be able to work, when a collection would be taken up to ship them out of the country, where they could end their days in some city hospital or almshouse.

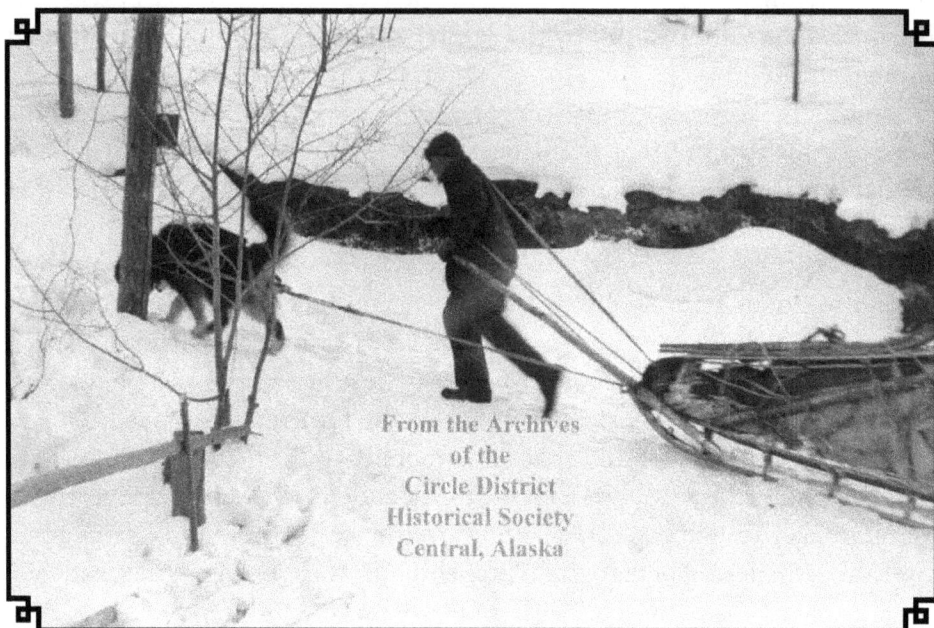

From the Archives
of the
Circle District
Historical Society
Central, Alaska

Ernest Behrens, prospector. Circle Hot Springs, Alaska.

Our culinary arrangements worked very smoothly, I had learned to make doughnuts so when my week in the kitchen arrived I always cooked a big batch to last through my term. One day while doing so, Crist and Bill Flanney were playing poker in the cabin. I had just put the last of my batch of doughnuts in a box, six dozen of them.

"There," I said, "that's seventy-two cakes, a dozen a day for six days, and I'll make a gingerbread for Sunday."

"How many did you say?" asked Bill. "Seventy-two? Just what I have won Crist, so I'll be going," and picking up the box he marched out of the door with it.

"Here!" I shouted. "Come back with those doughnuts!"

But Crist interposed sheepishly to tell me that he had been gambling with my doughnuts and had lost them all to Bill! How we roasted him all that week! Of course, I refused to make another batch, although I did relent and fix a spice cake for the Sunday meal.

With the long, dark days arriving toward Christmas, when the sun shone but an hour or so and finally disappeared altogether behind the southern hills, we lost all track of the time of the day. One might go to call on a neighbor and find him just going to bed at noon or getting up at midnight. When a person was sleepy he slept; when hungry he woke and ate.

With the disappearance of the sun in the south all life appeared to have ceased. Nature seemed to be holding her breath in a silence that had an element of dread and terror in it. The sky was an opaque mass of gloom. It was not cloud, it was not fog, there was no breath of wind, but out of the sullen heavens came dropping silently, slowly, steadily, and persistently, feathery, frost-like flakes of frozen vapor. They settled on tree, twig, and branch, loading them down with great wreaths and festoons of frost flowers that the least breath would have dissipated, but there they hung, and grew, and accumulated for weeks.

While the sun had been sinking into the southland, the moon had been climbing farther and farther north, until it reached its maximum during the shortest days of December. The Christmas full moon circled in a blaze of glory high up in the heavens, swinging, even at midday, far up above the treetops in the north, and for several days we had the unique spectacle of a moon that did not set.

Even Luna's sublime reflections grew pale and feeble in the brilliant light of the Aurora Borealis. Here in its birthplace, we saw this wonderful phenomenon in all its glory. Great billows and clouds of golden fire would start in the northeast, and twisting and rolling sweep rapidly overhead and southward. Streamers and tongues of lambent flame preceded and followed, as scouts or stragglers of the main body. Sometimes the display took on all the appearance of a tornado on the prairie, except that the inky black cloud was replaced with one of refulgent light. The storm nucleus was there, down from which trailed a rolling, twisting funnel-shaped tail that trailed along the ground, over treetops and up and down the sides of hill and mountains. I have even stood in the midst of it and been bathed in its stimulating, electrical flood. Some people with especially sensitive nerves are strongly affected by one of these peculiar displays. It is even accompanied by an audible sound ~ peculiar long drawn whish, far up overhead, something like the soft breath of a wind in the treetops, or like the rustling of a large silk flag in a gentle breeze. As one scintillating display would disappear, another wave would arise and pursue the former. Generally there were three waves

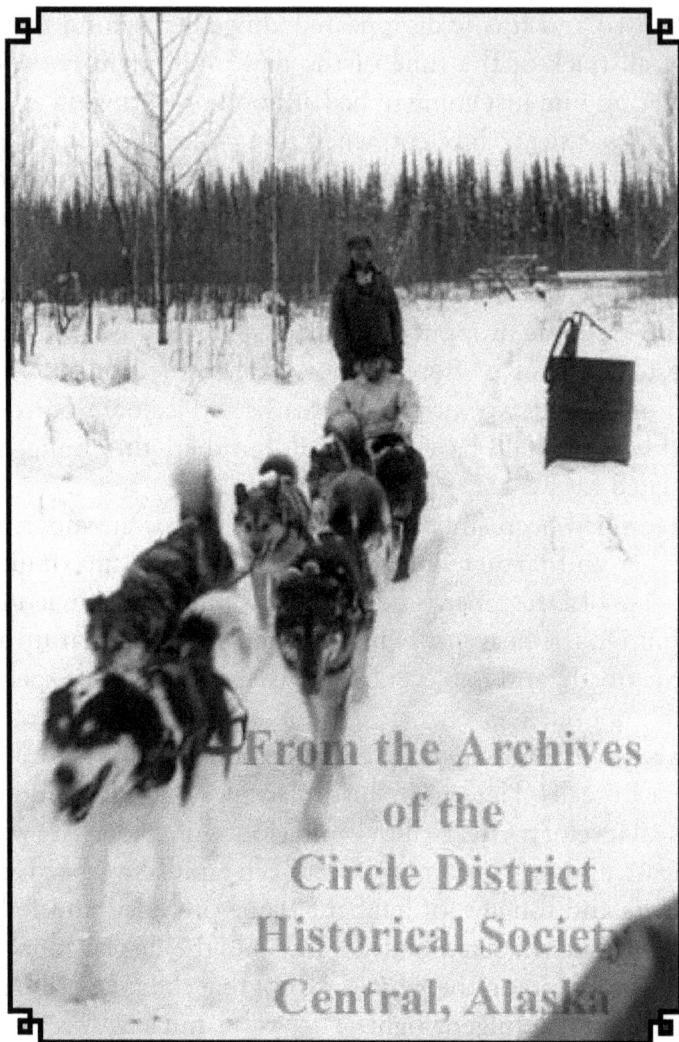

Dog team on trail.

in sight at the same time, one just starting, one in the zenith, and the last one disappearing. So brilliant was the light that one could see to read fine print while it lasted. It was an awesome sight that one never tired of viewing.

Even in this far away corner of the earth, Christmas was not forgotten. A Circle City grand ball was announced. There would be a turkey shoot, dog races, wrestling matches, and speeches by chosen orators. A poster got out in true circus style was posted on the door of the saloon announcing the prizes and names of the judges. The sled races, wrestling matches and running races were to take place in the morning, the shooting contest at noon when the sun, half an hour high, afforded the best light. The ball was to be in the evening, to be followed by toasts and a grand supper at midnight.

Word was sent out to all the neighboring Indians inviting them to attend and enter the contests. Their curiosity was greatly stimulated and elaborate preparations made. All their best finery was donned, and a gaily decorated procession passed by our door the day before Christmas. The Indians in town who had log cabins patterned after the white man's threw open their doors to their relatives and soon a thriving trade with the miners was established. The women had brought in loads of moccasins, mucklucks, mittens, parkas, socks, and robes. These they readily sold at good prices, and the proceeds were invested in bright ribbons and highly colored cotton handkerchiefs or cheap jewelry to be worn on the morrow's festive occasion.

The weather had been mild for several days and Frank Montgomery, our weather prophet, predicted it would remain so until the moon "fulled" on the twenty-seventh, when we were admonished to "look out for a change."

The dog races were to come off at ten o'clock. The course laid out was up River Street to McKenzie's cabin where the trail turned off into the slough, then up around the island and back to the starting point, a distance of three miles.

Six Indians and one white man, Frank Knight, had entered their teams for the race. Pitka and Soruska, the great men of the town Indians, brought up their finely rigged teams, nine gaunt, long-legged dogs, harnessed tandem, drawing handsome white birch toboggans ten or twelve feet in length. The front of each turned up and, brought back in a graceful curve, was painted and dyed in bright colors and decorated with two handsome foxtails. Ten-inch sides of rawhide, running the full length of the toboggans, served to hold in any article carried, or to prevent the loose snow from inconveniencing the driver. Each dog had a new mooseskin harness, consisting of collar, backband, and two traces, the latter being looped into pegs on the harness of the following dog. Gay ribbons and streamers completed the festive appearance of the teams.

Albert and Alexander from the fish camp above entered their respective teams, which, if not so gaily decked out, bid fair to make a stubborn contest for the prize. Two visitors from Medicine Lake were also among the contestants. All the Indians had toboggans, but Frank Knight brought out his freighting sled and team of eight heavy malemute dogs which, although strong and powerful as freighters, stood but little show in the race with the swift, wolfish dogs of the Indians.

The dogs danced and howled in impatience to be off, and it was with difficulty we could arrange them in line and keep them from indulging in a general fight before the word of start was given.

At last they were off, with shrill yells and cries from the Indians, cracking of whips, and ki-yi-ing from the dogs, as the sharp last stung and tingled their flanks and ears. A great crowd of observers had stationed themselves just where the trail led down the steep bank onto the slough. Here it was expected some mishap would occur, and it did. Pitka and Soruska were slightly in the lead, and neck and neck took the descent safely and swiftly swept up the smooth surface of the slough. Alexander, but little behind, followed their lead, but Albert's team in its endeavor to make a cutoff, shot over the twenty-foot bank and toboggan, owner and dogs were piled up in inextricable confusion in the soft snow below. The two teams from Medicine Lake, like sheep following their leader, plunged after them. The crowd caught the humorous side of the catastrophe and shouted and cheered in approval, and then rushed to the rescue, for a general dog fight had resulted from the spill, and it took the united efforts of a dozen men to separate the savage brutes. Indeed, Indian dogs were never happy unless quarreling with their neighbor or licking the wounds received in some former scrimmage.

Frank Knight's team, which from the start had no show to win, caught sight of a rabbit and belted the track, taking owner and sled, at a lively rate, among the thick fringe of willows lining the island, where they hung up until extricated by their owner and turned homeward.

The three leading contestants had now turned the head of the island were out of sight on the other side. Eagerly we watched for their reappearance. Then we saw them! Soruska was a little in the lead, Pitka second, and Alexander far behind. The Indians plied their whips and with cries in their native tongue urged the panting animals to greater exertions. Up the slope they came! Over humps and irregularities the toboggans leaped and flew from side to side with great bounds and jerks, and swept past the judges' stand. Soruska, half a length ahead of Pitka, was the winner of the prize, a keg of whiskey!

The wrestling match was won by Tom O'Brien, who by a dexterous turn laid Alexander the Indian champion on his back.

The turkey shoot had many contestants, for in this land of game every man prides himself on his marksmanship and the superiority of his rifle. In lieu of the feathered bird itself, a case of roast canned turkey had been offered as first prize, with a fine rifle for second. A target at just three hundred yards had been set up on the river, and for an hour Indians and white men vied with each other, each aspirant being allowed three shots. Jim Montgomery's score ranked highest and he proudly bore away the case of canned dainties, while Minuke's eyes sparkled over the .45-70 rifle he won as second price.

The ball in the evening and the supper that followed were a great success. Everyone agreed that it was the event of the winter, and although the ardent spirits circulated a little too freely, perhaps? "It was Christmas, and one must show his goodwill ~ pard!"

Chapter 11

Jacobi

The cold snap, predicted by Montgomery, came to hand and lasted six weeks. Lower and lower went the mercury until it froze solid. Forty, fifty, sixty below the spirit thermometer indicated. One morning even "painkiller" was frozen. The minus seventy point had been reached and still colder it grew. At eighty-five below the last alcohol thermometer burst, and we no longer had a record of the temperature.

At forty below the breath from mouth and nostrils issues as a white smoke, at fifty it whistles with a sharp crackling sound, and at sixty the result is intensified and the congealed moisture falls in little icy particles. At seventy and lower every breath is attended with sharp pains. Frequent hemorrhages follow any exertion and serious injuries to health may result. During these extreme cold spells, all are content to remain idle in cabin or tent. Nearly everyone carries a little bottle of quicksilver with him, and whenever it is cold enough to freeze that it is good policy to "lie by."

By the middle of February milder weather had set in and the old-timers prognosticated that the backbone of winter was broken. The sun was getting higher every day and while we were liable to have more cold spells, they would not be of long duration, nor so intense as the one we had just experienced.

Right after the Christmas holiday, several incidents took place in the camp and broke the monotony of the days. One was the trial and punishment of Jacobi. We had just finished our evening meal, with Kelley having prepared roast ptarmigan, frozen cranberry sauce (the berries for which were picked by the Indian women the previous fall), mushrooms, a pudding, and black coffee. Bullard had begun to tune up his violin, waiting for Kelly to finish his housework and produce his banjo before the regular evening concert began. Crist and I were engaged in a game of cribbage, when the door flew open and George Friend, the sheriff, burst into the room.

"Get a move on you fellows!" he shouted. "Chase yourselves down to Tom O'Brien's saloon. There's a big miners' meeting called. Alexander and a lot of his hunters are on the warpath," and without any further explanation he was gone to call the other camps in the vicinity.

A miner's meeting and a summons by the sheriff were not to be ignored. Hastily donning our furs we left our cabin and started for the rendezvous, a half mile distant. As we struck the trail we met Frank Montgomery and Lansing, who were camped near us.

"Know anything about what is up?" I queried of Lansing. "George Friend only said the Indians were on the warpath."

"He told us that someone had been stealing fish from "Alexander's cache on Seventh Mile," replied Lansing. "Cold, isn't it?"

Our breath whistled from our nostrils in a cloud of white steam, and ice piled up around our faces and on the long hairs on our parkas. A deadly chill struck us.

"About sixty below," announced Montgomery. "I looked at the glass when I stepped out."

O'Brien's saloon was nearly full when we arrived. The door swung open with a creak with every arrival, and a white cloud of fog rolled along the floor to the opposite walls and curled in fantastic wreaths around table legs and chairs, its moisture condensing on the flooring and lower logs of the building's walls until a sheen of ice coated them. The air above was blue with smoke, through whose murky dim half a dozen lamps struggled in vain to light up the interior of the room.

The bar was doing a brisk business. Nearly everyone of the one hundred and fifty miners present had taken at least one drink after coming in from the frozen outside. The roulette wheels and faro tables were in full swing and it was not until George Friend stepped upon a bench and called for order that the games ceased.

"Men!" shouted Friend, "here's Alexander from the Birch Creek Camp and he claims that his cache up on Seventy Mile has been robbed; what are you going to do about it?"

"Let's hear Alexander's story!" shouted back someone.

"Wait a moment," said Lansing, "we better do this in order. I move that Buckskin Miller act as chairman of this meeting."

"Second the motion," called a voice.

The motion was put and carried, and Buckskin Miller was escorted to the table near which a chair was placed for him.

"Now gentlemen, let us have a clerk," he announced. Handshaker Bob was chosen.

"We are now ready to proceed in an orderly manner," said Miller. "Alexander, come up here and tell your story."

The Birch Creek chief and half a dozen hunters had been standing quietly on one side during the preliminaries. None up to this time had spoken a word. But the old chief at Miller's invitation came forward and in broken English said, "Birch Creek Indians have cache on Seventy Mile ~ Ketchum all cache Seventy Mile ~ We go killum moose ~ killum bear Crooked Creek. Snow come ~ cold ~ freeze. Indians come back Seventy Mile to get fish, get robes, get snowshoes, get sleds ~ Seventy Mile cache broke open ~ fish gone ~ skins gone ~ snowshoes gone. White man take um; Birch Creek Indians very angry. Young men say, 'Go kill white mans.' Alexander more wise. He come tell white man. White man pay Indians ~ kill thief ~ all good friends then."

Not a word had been spoken by anyone else while the old chief was uttering his broken, laconic sentences.

"Alexander, how do you know it was a white man who robbed your cache?" questioned the judge. "Did you see him? Perhaps it was a wolverine or a pack of wolves that broke in."

"No wolves ~ no wolverine," replied Alexander shaking hard his head. "White man ~ me no see him ~ see tracks under cache. White man tracks ~ white man boots ~ three white mans," holding up three fingers. "Tracks show now ~ all hard ~ freeze um in mud!"

"It's a clear case, boys," said Miller turning to his audience. "The Indians don't make mistakes about such signs. We must hunt out the thief or thieves and punish them. Now to sift this thing down to where we can do something, let me ask, who came down past Seventy Mile this last fall?"

"I did," answered Missouri Bill. "Came down in September from Forty Mile. Saw the cache at Seventy Mile, but didn't stop. Don't know if it had been touched or not."

A score of others, including ourselves, gave similar testimony. In fact, nearly half the camp had come down that fall when the news of the new diggings at Circle had reached Forty Mile. Among the few who had camped at Seventy Mile on their way down, no one had noticed anything wrong with the Indians' cache.

"Well, let's get at it another way," said Miller. "I will ask who was the last man into camp before it froze up?"

A moment's silence, then someone shouted, "Old Maiden!"

Sure enough, some now remembered that Maiden with his two squaws had arrived just as the ice was jamming on the Yukon.

"Come up here, Maiden, and tell us what you know about it," invited the judge. "Did you look at the cache?"

"Yes, I did," replied Maiden. "Everything was in good order when we left. We got some skins that Alacacene, my woman, had left there in the spring."

As Maiden's woman belonged to the Birch Creek tribe, his word carried conviction with it. The robbery, if robbery it was, must have occurred later than Maiden's visit.

"Where's that Italian outfit?" shouted Tom-the-Turk. "They got in later than Maiden did. I helped pull them out of the ice."

To be sure, others now recalled this outfit of three men had got in just as the river froze up, and they were doubtless the very last arrivals from up river.

"What is the name of the parties?" inquired the judge.

"Jacobi! That is one of them." Someone volunteered.

"Come up here, Jacobi, and let us see you," called the chairman. No one answered or came forward.

"George, did you notify that outfit?" inquired Miller.

"Well, I sent Hans down that way," replied Friend. "I was up on the other side of town."

"Ja, I see him. I tell him to come up to miners' meeting," Hans answered.

"Notified but hasn't appeared" mused Miller. "That looks suspicious. Friend, suppose you go down and bring them here. Take a half dozen men with you and while you are about it you better look through their cache."

Quickly selecting a posse, Friend departed on his errand. A recess was taken awaiting their return. The bar did a rushing business, the roulette wheels commenced to turn, and the interrupted faro game was resumed.

Thirty anxious minutes passed, then a great stamping and talking was heard outside and the sheriff and posse came pushing into the room, bringing the three delinquent men with them. A Yukon sled loaded with a varied assortment of articles was brought in with them.

"Here's your men, judge!" shouted Friend. "And from the looks of things I guess we have the men we want. As sheriff of this town I accuse these men of stealing fish from Alexander and flour from Sid Wilson!"

"What!" excitedly exclaimed Wilson. "I haven't lost anything!"

"Just look at those sacks off flour on that sled," replied Friend. "Have you been selling flour to this outfit? I tried to buy flour off you and you had none to spare. How come if you are selling flour to Jacobi you wouldn't let your friends have any?"

"Go look in your cache and see if you are short," directed Miller.

Wilson flew out of the door and in a few minutes was back, answering, "Two sacks of flour are gone and a package of ten pounds of nails that I paid a dollar a pound for!"

"Here's your nails," announced Friend, holding up a package from the sled.

Miller rapped on the table. "Gentlemen, come to order. The sheriff has arrested these men and accused them of theft from Alexander and also from Sid Wilson. Whether they are guilty or not they must have a fair trial. I will appoint you, Lansing, as their attorney, and while I am selecting a jury you may confer with them."

Much against his will, Lansing drew the accused men over to one corner and carried on a murmured talk in which the Italian, Jacobi, seemed to grow excited and angry. Lansing appeared to be urging him to do something to which he refused.

"Are you ready, Lansing?" finally inquired the judge.

"All ready, your Honor," replied the attorney.

"Read the charge," Miller directed the clerk.

In formal words the accusation against the suspected men was read.

"What is the answer to the charge?"

"Not guilty."

"Bring your witnesses," directed the judge of the sheriff.

Alexander was the first put on the stand. The old Indian showed a shade of annoyance in being compelled to repeat his story, but he did so and no cross questioning could shake his testimony. The other Indians corroborated his evidence.

A bundle of dried fish, which had been found in the accused men's camp, was offered in evidence by the prosecution. Alexander shook his head when shown this exhibit.

"Me no know ~ dried fish him all alike ~ maybe mine ~ maybe not."

"Here are some moccasins," said Friend, handing over a pair from the sled.

These Alexander examined carefully, then showed them to his companions. They conversed together in their Indian gutturals. Then, pointing to Bear Paw, Alexander addressed the court. "Bear Paw's squaw make um these moccasins."

"Ugh," grunted Bear Paw.

"How do you know that she made them?" questioned Lansing.

Bear Paw pointed to a peculiar design worked in beads on the front of the foot. "Tatoosh make that, no odder woman do so."

"Call Sid Wilson," directed the judge next.

"Do you identify any of the articles brought from the cache of the accused men as yours?" inquired his Honor.

"I do," answered Wilson. "Two sacks of flour and that package of nails are mine."

"No questions," replied Lansing, answering a look from the judge.

"Put the prisoners on the stand. You first, Jacobi. Now Jacobi, tell us what you know about the cache at Seventy Mile," directed the judge.

"I not know Seventy Mile. I comma da boat down Yukon last fall, me and dese two men, Bill and Bob. Ice run-a like hell. We no stoppa at Seventy Mile ~ no see a Seventy Mile. I not know anything 'bout dis damm fool story of Birch Creek Indians!"

All the cross questioning could not shake his denials.

"How about those two sacks of flour and the package of nails that the sheriff found in your cache?" queried the judge.

"I buy 'em dat flour in Forty Mile ~ Jack McQuestion store. Dose nails, I bring a dose nails over de pass. No steal 'em. No steal 'em de flour, no steal 'em de fish, no steal 'em nothing!" vehemently declared Jacobi.

"All right, call the others, you first, Bob."

Bob Evans, a Nebraska boy, only twenty-one years old, was next put on the stand. He and Bill Jones were chums. They had reached Dyea late in the fall. There they had met Jacobi, and had packed over the summit together, and at Lake Lindeman, as was usual with the incoming men, had built a boat and floated down the river to Forty Mile, reaching that place shortly before the river closed in October. At Forty Mile, hearing of the new discoveries at Circle City, they laid in some supplies and hurried on down the river to the new camp. When questioned as to the truth of Jacobi's assertation that they made no stop at Seventy Mile, Bob manifestly was embarrassed, hesitated and looked at Bill and Jacobi. The latter was scowling at him.

"Your Honor, let me have a few more moments to consider some technicalities and to consult with my young clients before Bob answers that question," asked attorney Lansing.

It was granted and he drew the young man to one side where shortly a decision was made. When the question was repeated to Bob he said frankly,

"We did camp one night at Seventy Mile."

"It's a lie!" screamed Jacobi. "I tell-a you we no-a stoppa de boat -- run all a da time!"

"You shut your mouth!" yelled Friend. "You had had your say, now let the boy tell his story."

When questioning about the Indian cache, both boys confessed that they had at first examined it out of mere curiosity, never dreaming of molesting its contents, but Jacobi insisted that it was all right to help themselves to the fish and furs that they would need for the winter. Accordingly, all three of them did take some of the dried salmon and furs. The fish found in their cache had been stolen from the Indians, just as the old chief had said.

As for the flour and nails, both lads denied having any knowledge of them. They were sure neither article had been in the boat when they came down from Forty Mile, and they were equally positive in denying that they knew that the articles had been in their cache.

"That is all, your Honor," said Friend. "The stolen goods are found in the possession of the accused and I ask the jury for a conviction of all three of them."

Lansing, as attorney for the prisoners, made a short appeal. He acknowledged that the guilt of all was proven as far as the fish was concerned, but that Jacobi was alone guilty of the theft of the flour and nails. Moreover, the youth of the two of the number, who had been thoughtlessly led into the crime by Jacobi, called for clemency for them, especially as their testimony had been conclusive in fixing the greater guilt on Jacobi, where it belonged.

In charging the jury, the judge reminded them that the safety of, indeed the lives of, all the scattered miners and prospectors depended on the goodwill of the Indians. If the jury found that the accused had been guilty of theft from the natives, it was the duty of the jury to determine on a punishment severe enough to deter future offenses and that at the same time a punishment which should convince all the Indians that the white man would promptly punish his own people if they wronged the natives.

Without leaving their seats, the jury brought in a verdict of guilty. As was customary in miners' meetings, and in accordance with the instructions of the judge, the jury also fixed the penalty.

The two boys, Bob Evans and Bill Jones, were to be allowed sufficient supplies to keep them until the first boat went out in the spring, when they were ordered to leave the Yukon country and never return. The stolen goods were to be returned to their respective owners and the remainder of the outfit given to the Birch Creek Indians.

Jacobi was ordered to be driven from camp that night, without provisions, arms, or outfit of any kind. No one should succor him on pain of death. A hush fell over the crowded room as the dread verdict was pronounced by Frank Montgomery, the foreman of the jury. Those men knew that such verdict was death ~ yes, worse than death, but we all recognized that only a punishment of the greatest severity was adequate to meet the needs of the occasion.

The judge turned to Friend and briskly directed, "See that the verdict is carried out."

"Fall in men!" shouted the sheriff. "Make a double line from the door to the bank."

The door was thrown open and from the steaming, moist air of the saloon, out into the cruelly, cold, sixty below atmosphere, we streamed and lined up as directed. Here and there a torch flared out, dimly lighting up the grim, stern faces of the miners and the dark, impassive countenances of the Indians.

A moment's pause, and a last desperate struggle, and down between the lines came Jacobi, propelled by a man on either side, fifty ~ one hundred feet to the edge of the steep bank where, twenty feet below, under its eight foot shroud of ice and snow, glided the silent waters of the Yukon. A second's halt, a despairing cry, and the doomed man was precipitated over the bank to go slipping, cursing, falling to the ice below. Then silence ~ oblivion. The lines of men melted away and disappeared. Their work was done.

What of Jacobi? When the spring sun melted the snows, a group of prospectors starting out on their annual search for the yellow metal, found some scattered human bones ~ gnawed clean by the wolves ~ near the mouth of Seventy Mile. Had Jacobi expiated his crime where it was committed?

We never knew.......

Chapter 12
Potlatch

The other happening that occurred during that first long winter was the death of old Alexander, the chief of the Birch Creek Indians, and the potlatch to which we were invited to see his successor chosen.

For many years the warrior Alexander had led his people successfully on the hunt and to the fishing grounds where the winter store of dried salmon was cured against the long, cold winters of the Northland. But the Great Spirit had called and the old hunter had obeyed his call.

His body, wrapped in softest furs and incased in a big, birch bark casket, had been placed on the funeral cache. His favorite dog had been slain that he might accompany his master's spirit to the Happy Hunting Ground. Food had been provided for the journey; his canoe, sleds, and snowshoes were ready for his use, and for a full month the tribe remained quietly in camp, mourning the departed leader. But now when the moon of fat caribou came, a new chieftain must be chosen to lead the people. Among these northern Indians, the office of chieftain is not hereditary, but is purely elective.

Alexander left no son, but his brother, War Eagle, a tall, dark saturnine man of sixty years, was a candidate for his dead brother's office. He was known to be a successful hunter and trapper, but he did not look with a friendly eye on the white prospectors and miners, fast filling his country and driving out the game.

War Eagle was favored by the older men of the tribe, while the younger men put forth Bounding Moose, a young man just attaining his majority. Bounding Moose was on good terms with the white men, and they naturally hoped he would be chosen by his people.

So evenly matched were the two parties, that, following an ancient Indian custom, it was decided that a Potlatch must be held to settle the matter. Potlatch is a Chinook word and means "to give." The central idea of it is a distribution of gifts by a few persons to the many present whom they have invited. The giving is carried on to an extreme.

A person of equal importance with the chieftain was the Medicine Man. His province was to placate the evil spirits and keep them from exerting a malign influence on the tribe. Looked up to and feared as he was, the Medicine Man exacted a toll from all the hunters. The best of all the game, the choicest fish, and the warmest robes he claimed as his share. The daughter of the Medicine Man of the Birch Creek Indians was Wawa, the belle of the tribe, and it was rumored that she and Bounding Moose were lovers. A double incentive thus urged the young man on to win the coveted prize of the chieftainship, for it had been reported that the consent of the Medicine Man to the union of his daughter with Bounding Moose depended on the latter winning in the contest with War Eagle.

Bounding Moose gave an invitation to several of his white friends, and on the afternoon of the eventful day, we left our cabins at three p.m. and took the trail leading to the left bank of the Yukon to the Indian village. The sun was just disappearing below the southwestern hills. The snow creaked and crackled under our snowshoes, and the frost crystals on the willows, fringing the river's bank, sparkled and glittered in the fading sunlight.

Long before we reached the Indian camp, we could smell the pungent smoke of the campfires, and catch the fragrance of roasting meats, filling the evening air. On rounding the bend just below the village we caught sight of the fires, gleaming through the trees, and could see the moving figures of the natives, passing to and fro.

The Indian village was situated in one of the beauty spots so often found along the Yukon. Just where the river opens on the Great Yukon Flats, it is confined to one channel, half a mile wide. On the far side the cliffs rise sheer and rugged one thousand feet, against whose bases the river foamed and fretted, with many an eddy and back-current during the salmon season. On the near bank, where the lodges were located, the river, by successive overflows during high water, had built up a bank or levee of silt, free of underbrush, but covered with the carpet of moss so universal in this northern country.

Heavy-coned spruces and white paper birches covered this natural park, and it was here the Indians had their winter homes. These were substantial log structures, chinked with moss, and banked and covered with earth. Comfortable enough in the extreme cold, they were much too small for any large gathering such as now took place, so it was necessary to resort to the open air, where a degree of comfort was secured by large open fires.

The banquet was well underway when we arrived. Over the fires, huge pots were bubbling and seething, and from their contents the Indian women were ladling out portions of meat or fish, in birch bark dishes, which they served to the assembled crowd. On beds of glowing coals, juicy moose and caribou steaks were sending out appetizing odors on the frosty air. We were speedily helped to a generous portion of the eatables, and did full justice to them; the bracing air and our long walk were good preparations for such a hearty meal.

The men and voters of the tribe were seated in a circle around a large central fire; back of them clustered the women and children; and farther out among the trees we could see the gleaming eyes of the ever-hungry Indian dogs. Bones and scraps of food were tossed to them, and many a sharp fight took place among the savage brutes. For an hour the feasting continued, until finally we could eat no more.

Then, the men of the tribe lighted their pipes and signified that they were ready for the serious business of the evening. Within the circle of men were two large heaps of gifts, and by their respective goods the two candidates took their stand.

War Eagle, as the older, addressed the assembly first. He gave an impassioned eulogy of the dead chieftain; praised his virtues, his skill and sagacity. He reminded the tribe of their prosperity under Alexander's leadership, and then skillfully touched on his own qualifications to fill the office. He was the brother of Alexander, and promised to carry out all his relative's plans and wishes. Then, selecting a beautiful silver fox skin robe, he presented it to the Medicine Man, and in a graceful speech complimented him on his skill in keeping the evil spirits away from the tribe and prophesied even greater results in the future. This done, War Eagle returned to his place and Bounding Moose had his turn.

His eulogy of the dead Alexander was no less fulsome than had been that of War Eagle; but now a younger man was needed to lead the hunters and fishermen, he told them.

"Who," he inquired, "as well as Bounding Moose knew where the bear made her den, or the moose hid her young, or the trail the fat caribou would take when returning from her summer pasture in the northland? Who as well as Bounding Moose could get the tea, tobacco, or sugar from the white man, or the red calicoes for the women, or the beads and looking glasses that they might adorn themselves and show their charms to their husbands and sweethearts?"

Bounding Moose's first gift was a repeating rifle he had purchased from the white traders. This was presented to the Medicine Man.

Then followed alternate gifts. First War Eagle, then Bounding Moose gave

72

in turn, until the whole circle of men had each received a present, its value proportioned to the recipient's standing in the tribe. None of the women were offered a gift, but among the various presents given by the candidates were many articles that, undoubtedly, were intended to be passed over to the fair ones.

War Eagle's presents were all homemade, either by himself or by his wife, Tatsutinita. There were robes, furs, moccasins, snowshoes, sleds, canoes, dogs, fishing gear, all useful and well appreciated articles.

Bounding Moose's gifts were different. Meats, skins, and furs of the hunt were in abundance, but the larger part, and the most highly prized of his gifts, had come from the white traders. Beginning with the rifle which he gave to the Medicine Man, Bounding Moose followed with axes, hatchets, knives, beads, looking glasses, tobacco, pipes, tea, sugar, bright calicoes and ribbons. These latter were passed over to the women, as it had been intended they should be, and soon an audible murmur of the name of Bounding Moose could be heard from the gathered circle. Every gift was accompanied with a graceful allusion to some well-known and flattering quality of the recipient. Bear Paw was reminded of his fight with a ferocious bear, by which he had acquired his name. Lynx Eye was told of his keenness of vision. Swift Water was complimented on how he could guide a canoe amid the rapids of the Yukon. Raven Wing, White Owl, and Red Fox ~ none were forgotten.

At last the rounds had been made and the candidates awaited the decision of the voters. But none came. There were yet gifts to be given and received, and the minds of the Indians were still under a cloud. Again the process of distribution was repeated and continued until at last both Bounding Moose and War Eagle stood before their constituents with empty hands. Of the great heaps of gifts, nothing now remained with the former owners; all had been passed over into other hands, and now came the moment to decide between the two rivals.

As War Eagle had made the opening speech, as befitted his years, he now made his final appeal. "My brothers of the Birch Creek," he began. "War Eagle has given you all his possessions, that he might show you, by his generosity, that his heart is warm toward you, that whatever War Eagle has will always be yours, and whatever War Eagle does, he will do to make his brothers happy. Who so well as War Eagle is fitted to be the leader of his people?" Then in dignified silence the old hunter waited until Bounding Moose had spoken.

Said the latter, "My brother, the War Eagle, has told you he has given

73

you all he owns; that is true, but present for present Bounding Moose had given you equal or greater ones than has War Eagle, and now War Eagle is done, but Bounding Moose has still presents for his brothers."

Stooping, he threw aside a caribou skin and uncovered two bottles of whiskey that he had obtained from the white traders. Holding them high in the air, one in each hand, he exclaimed, "See, brothers of the Birch Creek: See the wisdom water of the White Man. Let my brothers drink of this wisdom water and they will know that Bounding Moose is the man they would have to lead them in the footsteps of the dead Alexander."

Eager hands stretched out to grasp the much coveted firewater and the bottles passed from hand to hand around the circle, with gurgles of satisfaction. When at last they were returned to Bounding Moose, one of them had a small portion of the fiery liquor remaining in it. Holding the bottle in his hand, a spirit of malice crossed his countenance, and approaching the motionless War Eagle, he held out the bottle, saying, "Let my brother, War Eagle, drink of the wisdom water and see if he has not some other present yet that he has been keeping for himself."

The tones and words would have been a mortal insult under other circumstances, but a Potlatch gift may not be refused. Gravely raising the bottle to his lips, the old warrior drained the entire contents, then handing the bottle back to the donor, he remained in profound meditation for a moment. Then turning to Bounding Moose he said, "I thank you my brother; the Bounding Moose is right. War Eagle now sees clearly that he had forgotten a present that he should have given his brother. I will go get it."

So saying he strode out of the circle into the group of women, and grasping his wife by the hand he drew her into the midst of the men. The old woman of sixty winters was bent and haggard, her face hideously tattooed in the manner of the older natives. She was nearly toothless and showed strongly the ravages of time and hardships. Holding her there, beside him, War Eagle addressed the tribe: "See, brothers, here is Tatsutinita, the wife of War Eagle. Where is the woman who can prepare the furs like Tatsutinita? Who can cure the red salmon as she can? Who can catch the white rabbit or pick the berries as well as Tatsutinita? Who as well as Tatsutinita can keep the fires warm in her husband's lodge? And is it well that War Eagle should have a woman like Tatsutinita when he looks into the lodge of his brother, Bounding Moose, and sees it is empty, the fires cold, no woman to prepare his food, or dress his furs, or cure his fish? No, War Eagle gives Tatsutinita to Bounding Moose; she is his woman!" And leading her over to Bounding Moose, he placed her hand in that of his astounded rival.

The divorce, according to Indian customs, was legal, and as the transaction was a Potlatch gift it could not be refused. The boomerang of the wisdom water had returned to its giver! The Indians caught the subtle humor of the affair, and in a burst of enthusiasm, shouted, "War Eagle wins! War Eagle wins! War Eagle is our Chief!"

The old warrior, in dignified words, accepted the gift of office, promising to lead them in successful hunts, and wisely guide them in their dealings with the white man. Then turning to the Medicine Man, he said, "Father, the men of the Birch Creek Indians have asked War Eagle to be their Chief; he has accepted, but when he looks into his lodge he finds it empty; the fires are cold, there is no woman to prepare his meals, or dress his furs, or follow him on the trail. Is it well that the Chief of the Birch Creek Indians should thus be alone? Speak to Wawa that she may come to him. She will be welcome."

And the Medicine Man, turning to his daughter, said, "Wawa, a Chieftain calls; let your moccasins be found beside his campfire!"

We returned to our cabins impressed with the Indians' process of election!

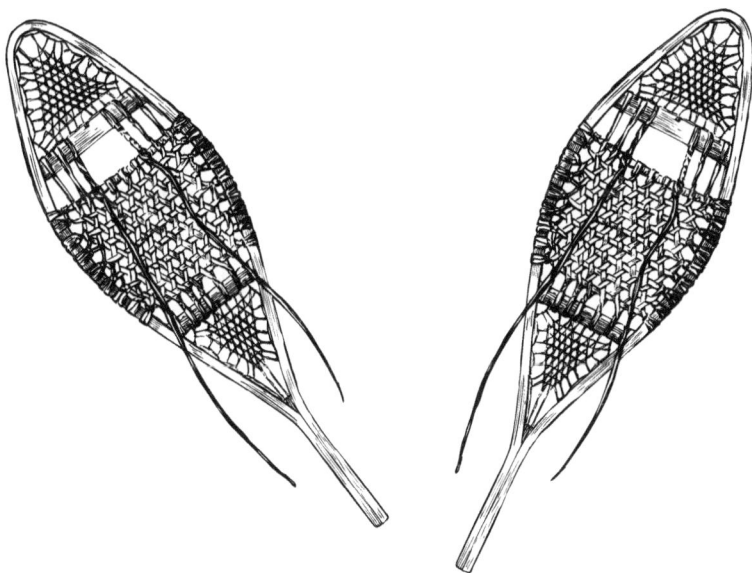

Chapter 13
The Ice Worm Tale

There were a few old sourdoughs in camp, Cassiar miners and some who had wintered on the Yukon when there was nothing but the fur trade to attract one, who delighted to sit around the fire in Tom O'Brien's saloon and spin yarns to us cheechakos. One of these men was Chris Sonnikson. A characteristic story of his was the one about the ice worm. Giving it as nearly as I can in his own words, it ran as follows:

"One winter Kate and me was camped at the mouth of Stewart River. Kate was my squaw, ya know. The summer fishing had been poor and our stock of dried fish was all gone by Christmas. Then too, the caribou run had missed. I got one moose early in the fall but that meat was about done too. Generally we could depend on rabbits to help us out if we got short, and the Stewart might to have been a good rabbit country, but this year was the year the rabbits 'went to their mamas' as the Indians say. That is, once in seven years there comes an epidemic that sweeps off all the rabbits, leaving hardly enough for seed. This was an epidemic year too.

"Things looked pretty tough and I said to Kate that I guessed we would have to eat the dogs to keep from starving to death. I remember it was an unusually cold winter too. Didn't have any thermometer but I know I had to bring my quicksilver into the cabin to thaw it out and ya know quick freezes at forty-two, so think it must have been down in the fifties or sixties, perhaps worse."

"One day Kate had gone down to the water hole after a pail of water and she come running back. 'Come quick, look Chris! Ice worm he come, plenty eat!'

"I hurried down and sure enough I could hear the worms boring and cutting the ice all around. The dogs too had spotted them and I saw old Catchuck make a grab at the head of a worm a good yard long and big around as a sausage. You bet we lost no time in getting our share and back at the cabin we had a square meal! The worms were so fat they would fry themselves. We lived high all the rest of the winter and the dogs came out the fattest in the spring I ever saw them do. The funny part about it though was that when the spring break-up came, the ice was so tangled and tied up it couldn't run out but had to lie there until it melted!"

The old-timers always expected the audience to set up the drinks after one of these yarns, and they were never disappointed.

Chapter 14

A Moose Hunt on the Yukon

Before winter was over, fresh meat in camp had been getting pretty scarce. A few fortunate ones who had gone up to the Yukon in the fall and floated back with moose killed near the river still had a supply, but the rest of us had exhausted our stock of both meat and fish. I decided to ask the Indians about hunting for a moose. I spoke to Pitka about it. He shook his head, and said, "No good ~ no wind. Bime bye wind blow ~ me ketchum moose then."

I did not quite understand what he meant at the time, but I subsequently learned that in the winter the moose's sense of hearing is so acute that it is impossible to approach one on the snow unless there is a wind blowing. On the Yukon Flats, from October until February, not a breath of air is stirring; the frost feathers accumulate and grow and swing from the bending spruces in great festoons and wreaths. A cracking stick can be heard a mile, and so it is almost impossible to stalk any game at this season. I wished to witness the Indians' method of hunting and after much persuasion and bribing, I induced Pitka to let me accompany him on his next expedition.

"Next moon ~ sun get high ~ wind blow ~ me ketchem plenty moose," he announced laconically.

It was the middle of February. Just after the cold snap had let up, Pitka and Soruska decided the time had come to hunt the moose. So one bright, crisp morning they loaded their belongings into two large toboggans, whose capacity was crowded to the utmost with their bedding, household items, guns and ammunition, as well as my own robes and private stock of provisions.

I soon realized that the men were leaving all of their squaws to bring on the teams and papooses; we struck out ahead following the miners' trail to Birch Creek as far as the mouth of Crooked Creek, which we reached just at dusk, having made no stop for dinner. I, fortunately, had provided myself with a cold lunch of doughnuts and bacon, otherwise I could have hardly made the walk of thirty-two miles. As it was, I was both lame and weary from the unusual exertion, and I hailed with delight the sight of a tent at this point as something providential. This belonged to Old Jerry Cummings, a seasoned sourdough who had gone on a little camping expedition on his own a few days earlier. He invited me to supper and after a hearty meal I agreed to share his tent for the night.

The Indians did not have any tents. They built a rousing fire on which their supper of dried fish and tea was prepared, then on a makeshift bed of boughs they huddled together under their robes to pass a most uncomfortable night, judged from a white man's standpoint.

In the morning, Pitka explained that we must leave the miners' trail that we had followed the previous day. We were to strike out for Medicine Lake, ten miles distant, which was to be the scene of our hunting operation.

Snowshoes were donned, and following the lead of Pitka we struck off single file across the dreary swamps and flats whose snow-covered surface stretched miles away to the hills on the farther side of the valley. Small, stunted spruces rose here and there, their sickly, half-dead appearance testifying to their unequal struggle for existence on the frozen bosom of the tundra which even the midsummer sun only could succeed in thawing a foot or two. Occasionally we crossed and re-crossed Crooked Creek, and its banks for a short distance were lined with a fringe of larger spruces.

Moose signs were abundant, but our guide paid no attention to them. Little knolls or ridges of higher ground were pointed out as favorable spots for moose to be hidden. These higher places were fringed with willows, beyond were white birch and aspen, favorite food for the moose.

The dogs readily followed the trail made by our snowshoes, and the native toboggan proved its superiority to a sled in carrying a heavy load over a poorly beaten trail.

At Medicine Lake, which we reached by the middle of the afternoon, Pitka had a barabara which had been used many times on similar occasions. It was a circular house with four foot walls of logs and moss on which the rafters rested, their points all meeting at an apex in the roof. Moss and earth covered all except a hole in the center through which smoke from the fire could escape. A covered passageway led into the interior of the structure. Around the walls was a raised shelf, three feet wide which served as beds, seats, or table as the occasion required. The walls and rafters were stained with smoke from former fires which had been built on the ground in the center to provide warmth and means for cooking. Light was admitted through a bladder-skin window inserted in the roof. This barabara had been the winter home of Pitka and his family before the white miners came into the country.

After we had all had our meal (I was eating my own provisions), I was assigned a place on the circular shelf for sleeping, where, rolled in my robes and blankets, I was soon asleep and dreamed of killing a gigantic moose.

The hunters were to be up and away early the next morning if the weather were favorable. At the first streak of daylight the Indians were astir. Breakfast was quickly dispatched and we sallied forth on our snowshoes. A fair wind from the northwest promised a successful day.

The Indians led the way around the north shore of the lake where the fringe of willows and birches indicated good feeding ground for moose. The air was keen and sharply nipped our exposed ears or nose. A brisk gait kept our blood circulating and for an hour we kept steadily on without seeing fresh signs, although old ones were abundant.

At last, just as the first beams of the sun were peeping over the southern hills, Pitka pointed to unmistakably fresh indications. A couple of moose had passed shortly before, feeding on the low bushes as they went. A cow and her last year's calf, the Indians pronounced. The course we took was against the wind, for the moose when feeding or traveling almost always take the wind from the front. Consequently, by following their trail, we could approach without fear of their getting our scent and the brisk wind blowing would prevent the creak of our snowshoes reaching them. To my surprise, the Indians used no unusual precautions but pushed ahead at a rapid pace for about a mile, when Pitka stopped and held up his hand for silence. The trail had turned abruptly to the right and entered a thick bunch of spruces along which we had been following for the last three hundred yards.

"Moose sleep now. Him down in there," whispered Soruska, pointing back toward the center of the trees.

Turning square around in our tracks, we retraced our steps until we came opposite the lower end of the group of trees, then striking off at right angles to our trail, Pitka led the way for a couple of hundred yards and stopped. This last maneuver was thus parallel to and three hundred yards below the one made by the moose when they turned off to sleep, as prophesied by Soruska.

"Take off snowshoes now. Make no noise," directed Pitka.

The snow, which as yet had not been settled by the sun, came nearly up to our waists and rendered our progress extremely difficult. Slowly and laboriously we forced our way up through the trees, each step was carefully planted so no snapping of a dead limb might alarm the game that the Indians seemed confident was close. Intervening limbs were carefully moved aside and each inch of snow in front and to the right and left was closely scrutinized. Fully half an hour was used in moving ahead one hundred yards.

I had begun to be skeptical and was likewise growing impatient at the delay when Pitka held up his hand and pointed ahead and slightly to the right of our position. At first I could see nothing that looked like a moose, and glanced questionably at Pitka. Following the direction of his outstretched finger, I finally discerned a grayish patch upon the snow and not over fifty yards away. It was the back of a moose, which was lying down, the snow hiding all but the upper part of its body. But where was the other one? We peered vainly on all sides and Soruska even made a detour of several yards in hopes to locate it, but unsuccessfully.

"We shoot 'em this one ~ maybe you shoot 'em odder one!" said Pitka.

I agreed to this arrangement and stood with rifle ready. Two sharp cracks of the Indians' guns brought the moose to her feet with a snort, and with a great crashing of branches she made off through the trees, followed by a shower of bullets as fast as the Indians could work their repeaters.

At the first fire the second moose, a yearling buck, had sprung up from its bed seventy-five yards to the right of us. The spruce trees were open in that direction and for one moment it stood bewildered and enabled me to get in a shot through the shoulder. With a squeal it dropped to the ground, but instantly sprang up and made off. My second shot missed it and before I could fire again it was out of sight!

I wondered what I should do next, but fortunately the Indians now brought up the snowshoes, and putting on my pair I determined to follow the one I had wounded, cautiously, while my companions started off after theirs. I followed the blood-sprinkled trail five hundred yards through the open snow, when it entered another willow patch. Pushing through the interlacing branches I almost fell over the prostrate body. The moose made an ineffectual attempt to rise, but a shot through the head put it out of pain.

Hearing the report of my gun, the Indians hurried up to see me, they having found and dispatched the old moose. While engaged in skinning and cutting up the game, the squaws with the toboggans and dog teams made their appearance. They had followed at a safe distance behind until the report of the guns informed them that the game had been found.

While they were loading the toboggans and putting the rest of the meat on a cache to be safe from wolves and other marauding thieves, I retraced my steps as I was curious to learn how the Indians had hit upon the exact location of their game. I found that after the moose had turned off at right angles to their trail, they had turned back describing nearly a complete circle, coming back inside the loop so formed to sleep. Had we followed directly on their trail we would have passed completely around them, and when to the windward of their position would have given them warning of our presence. But the superior sagacity of the Indians had outmatched their cunning and allowed us to come upon them in their rear and only unguarded point.

Back at the barabara, a fire was kindled and over this pots filled with fresh meat were soon bubbling and simmering. Every portion of the game had been saved, even the entrails, which, gorged with a half-digested mass of willow and birch twigs, was considered a great delicacy. One pot was filled with portions of the entrails and was carefully tended by the oldest squaw. Declining their invitation to eat with them, I soon had a juicy steak of my own broiling on the coals!

The Indians are fond of black tea and on this occasion tea and meat, both in prodigious quantities, were devoured, the feast being prolonged far into the night. It is always a feast or a famine with the Indians, and when the former, their capacity to store away eatables is simply marvelous.

Knowing that the natives would pass the next day in idleness, I rose early determined to stalk a moose alone. I had scarce gone one thousand yards when I crossed the fresh tracks of a monster animal. This I followed for upward to two miles until it came out on the banks of Crooked Creek, near where we had crossed two days previously. Here the moose had gone down upon the ice and followed the surface of the frozen stream. But here I noticed a new and alarming addition to the trail. A pack of wolves, not less than a dozen in number, had come upon the scent and struck off in pursuit.

I debated a few moments whether to follow or not. The deep snow had rendered the wolves half starved and consequently dangerous. On the other hand, I might have an opportunity to secure several fine wolf skins. This last made me decide and I followed the now well-beaten trail down the creek.

For the first half mile the moose had proceeded leisurely, cropping the willows along the bank, unconscious of his pursuers. I could even determine when he first got warning of their approach; I saw where he had turned around in his tracks, facing upstream until he either saw or scented his enemies, then wheeling he made off in great gigantic bounds. But the moose does not run far.

In the summer it always takes to the nearest water, where it is safe, striking dead the wolves if they venture to approach it there. For the same reason the moose will stand at bay in the winter on the ice of lake or river.

A confused noise of snarls and howls apprised me that the quarry was at bay not far off. It came from a spot just around the bend in the stream. Cautiously working my way across the neck of land, screened by the trees and underbrush, I came unperceived upon the savage scene. There stood the largest moose I had ever seen! Surrounded by his foes, he was stamping his hoofs in rage, and over and anon would make a rush at his enemies. The pack made several ineffectual dashes at him, only to be met by a bold front, and were driven off by the deadly hoofs; two of their number with broken backs were howling in misery.

I was filled with admiration at the brave resistance made by the noble animal and had resolved to interfere in his behalf. Then, suddenly, the wolf pack divided, and I waited to see what new developments were to take place. Both packs made a simultaneous rush. The one in front was boldly met and driven back, one of its numbers paying the penalty with his life, but before the moose could turn on those in his rear, the wolves had hamstrung him and with a hideous cry of agony he sank upon his haunches, unable to support his weight. With yells of triumph, the remaining wolves flung themselves upon the disabled monarch and in a second his throat was torn open and the struggle was over. Then my trusty rifle spoke and two more of the pack fell its victims before the rest got out of reach. Five fine black pelts rewarded me for the loss of the moose, and a liberal dose of strychnine applied to the mangled carcass assured me of more as we found on our return on the morrow.

Chapter 15
#39 On Mastodon
Spring, 1895

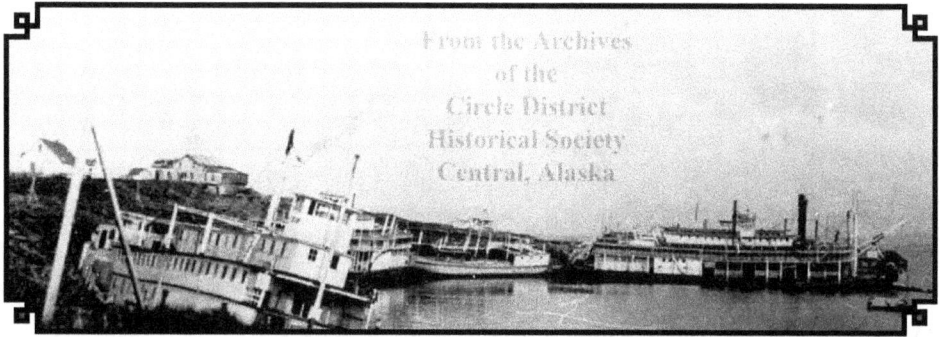

Yukon River.

When I had returned to my own camp after the moose hunt, I found that Jim had made arrangements with Sid Wilson to freight our outfits from the Twelvemile Cache to the mines. We were to get the stuff to the cache and Sid would pick it up there. Wilson was in the freighting business and Jim agreed to pay for the hauling with wood which we could cut at four dollars per cord. We welcomed the opportunity for we were already getting tired of the enforced winter idleness. We all sallied out with axes and attacked the standing spruces. By this time the extreme cold weather had made the wood as brittle as glass. Cut in four-foot lengths and the logs quartered, it did not take long to put up a cord of wood. The only trouble was the job did not last long enough, but we welcomed the work even though it was of short duration.

We next decided to haul our outfits to the Twelvemile Cache. Both sleds were loaded with about five hundred pounds each. The trail was already getting well beaten as other miners had begun hauling their outfits also. We had to cross a ten-mile-wide tundra. This tundra is virtually a swamp in the snow. Under the snow is moss and it is comparatively level and smooth going. Here and there are little gulches or drainage ditches. Jim set the pace and we forged rapidly along. We covered the distance to the cache within four hours. Emerging on Birch Creek and coming to the opposite bank, we found a veritable village of caches all loaded with miners' provisions.

We selected some trees, cut them off ten feet from the ground, laid a platform, and hoisted our goods into place. We then returned home.

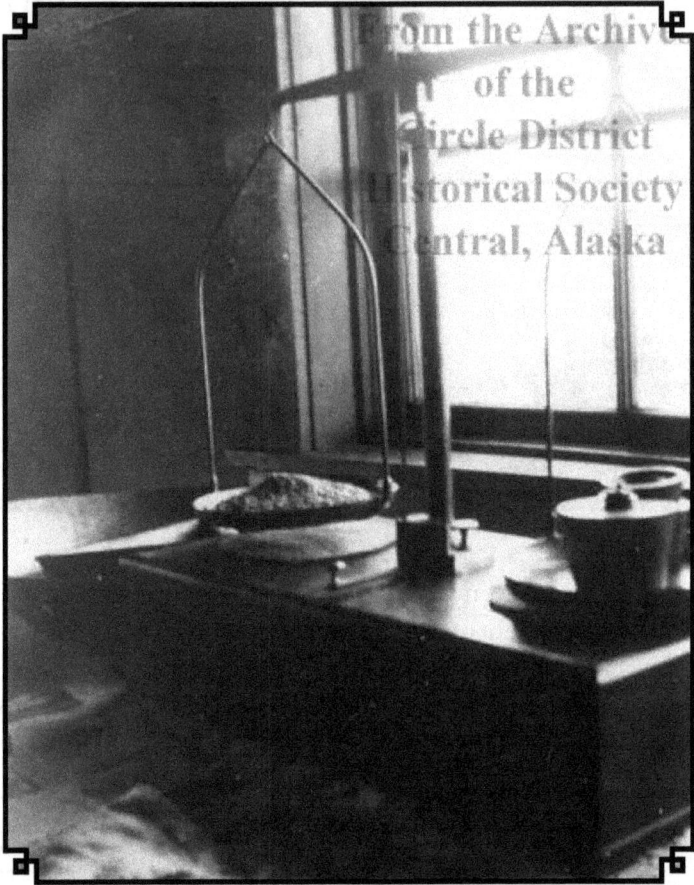

Gold scale with gold.

"We'll take a bigger load tomorrow," said Jim, but neither tomorrow or the next day did we take any load to our cache. It was Crist's day to cook and I heard him groaning and growling while he was rattling the stove building a fire.

"What's the matter, John?" I asked.

"Oh, these legs of mine are so stiff I can hardly walk!" he complained.

"So are mine," said Kelley, and on trying to rise both Jim and I found we were practically cripples. Our leg muscles and ankles under the unusual strain of yesterday were cramped and sore. Frank Montgomery looked in that morning and discovered our plight.

"You boys overdid it the first day," he volunteered. "You ought to have made short runs a few days before you made a long one. Oh well, rest a couple of days and you will be all right."

We did rest up and had no more trouble when we resumed the rest of the hauling. At the end of February we bade good-by to our town cabin and with our beds, tent, stoves, and remainder of our provisions started on our seventy mile haul to Mastodon where lay the claim we had purchased.

We camped the first night at the Twelvemile Cache, where we found the provisions we had left there were all safe. Selecting some among them such as we would need for immediate use until Sid Wilson brought up the remainder, we moved forward by easy stages toward the mountains where our prospects lay.

Through the wide, flat tundra country we first had to cross Birch Creek and its tributary, Crooked Creek, where I had been with the Indians on the moose hunt. Crooked Creek wound back and forth in great sweeps and oxbow bends. Eventually we advanced toward the narrow opening in the hills where Crooked Creek emerged upon the tundra land. These low rolling foothills were densely wooded, though the timber was small. I noticed especially the white paper birch that gave the larger stream its name. This birch with its oily papery bark made the best of firewood. Even green birch burns well, and a handful of the bark stripped off the trees makes a fierce fire that will burn even if wet. A plan adopted by us and practiced by all wise mushers was to fill our Yukon stove, after the fire was out, with birch bark and kindling so that just touching a match to them we had a rousing fire ready for any emergency.

Cold and sharp and clear were the days. How Jim did delight to get up in the morning and rouse the rest of us to eat our bacon and beans and drink strong coffee! The days were getting perceptibly longer, and wildlife in the woods became more abundant. More than once we crossed fresh moose tracks. Rabbits abounded and we often had one to fry with our bacon. The rowdy, though exceedingly beautiful, big, Whiskey Jack or Moosebird fearlessly invaded our camp, stealing any loose article; pieces of soap seemed a special delicacy to it! We saw Willow Ptarmigan, and later as we reached higher altitudes Rock Ptarmigan were abundant. There was also a species of grouse, the Blue Spruce Grouse, which was known by the miners as "fool hens." The Raven of the Arctic with its hoarse call hovered nearby, ready to pounce on any remnants left from the camp. Even a small member of the Finch family, a little yellow-breasted Canary, chipped and twitted in the spruce thickets. The large, tufted horned arctic Owl sailed noiselessly through the trees looking for some unwary rabbit, and even red squirrels came out and chattered at us from overhanging limbs. It seemed strange that so much life could have existed through the long, cold winter.

Foxes and wolves were more or less abundant and occasionally the track of a wolverine was noticed. These latter animals fortunately were not plentiful as they were most destructive to the caches of provisions, tearing up and destroying what they could not eat. So far we had not seen any caribou, the wild reindeer of the north, but the season was too early for the northward migration of the big herds.

Discovery on Mastodon was reached one evening. Here was considerable activity. Pat and Jack, friends from camp, were erecting cabins and had men at work a few miles below, sawing out lumber for sluice boxes.

"I guess that is something we will have to do," said Jim, "if we find pay on our ground."

We had purchased number 39 above Discovery. As there were ten claims to the mile, it meant our ground was four miles further up the creek. The trail grew steeper as we toiled upward. Two miles above Discovery we passed the last timber. Nothing but willows and small alders and the ever present Labrador tea plant remained.

"Humph," said Kelley, "poor prospect for a fire and it is my week to cook!"

"Have to haul a load of wood up from timber line," Jim explained, "and it is my week to get the wood!"

"How about water?" asked Crist.

"Melt snow until the thaw comes," I replied.

We finally pitched our tent on the claim, which we located with some difficulty, but eventually found a blazed stake with number 39 scrawled on it, and later located number 40 above it in like manner. The first thing we had to do was to get up some wood for fires, both to burn in the stove and for thawing out the frozen ground where we would sink a shaft to prospect our property. To go back down the gulch two miles, cut a log or two, load our sleds with it and get it to our camp took a good half day and two trips a day gave even Jim all the exercise he wanted! After a few loads on hand, we divided our work. Crist and I took over the job of wood hauling and Jim and Kelley looked after the camp and began sinking a shaft.

As the ground was frozen solidly, the method adopted was to build a good fire, let it burn overnight, then in the morning shovel out the thawed soil, build another fire and repeat the process from day to day until bedrock had been reached. It was a slow process. About one foot was considered a good thaw and Jim used near a cord of wood to a fire.

"Gracious!" said Crist, "I see where we spend the rest of the winter and all of spring as lumber jacks!"

We wished we had dogs to help us on the hard pull up the gulch, but it took lots of bacon and flour to feed dogs and our provisions were not ample enough to warrant us affording dogs, so we had to content ourselves with our own labor.

Jim next started another shaft about twenty feet from the first one and later a third. The idea was to crosscut the gulch so, if the first shaft did not locate pay dirt, one of the others might, or if all shafts showed good results we would know we had a wide and valuable pay streak. We could hardly wait to find out! The first shaft was down to about ten feet. Jim began twirling a gold pan in a wooden box of water we had made for that purpose.

"Find anything, Jim?" we asked, crowding around him as he carefully examined the residue in the pan.

"Nothing but a little black sand," he said holding up the pan for inspection.

"Oh well, we aren't down anywhere near bedrock yet," Crist advised consolingly. But a week later as we toiled up with our loads, Jim held up a pan and pointed excitedly to a little line of bright, shining yellow particles.

"Struck it sure!" he cried, "and not reached bedrock yet!"

We gathered around the pan and poked the little scales of yellow metal.

"How much?" demanded Crist. "A dollar?"

"Oh, no." Jim replied, "not that much, but we can weigh it. Get the gold scales, Kelley, let's find out!"

Kelley got the scales, a little pair of balances with brass scoops to hold the dust on one side and the weights in the other. Kelley put a half ounce weight in one pan. We greeted that with a laugh for we all knew that half an ounce meant eight dollars. Then Crist tried a grain weight which was about five cents. Even that was too much! Half a grain was a little too light. We decided our gold was worth just about three cents, but that was promising as no doubt nearer bedrock the pay would be richer.

The next day the pans showed better yet. One pan produced ten cents and in the second one Jim tried there was a beautiful little solid piece, a miniature nugget that weighed out at twenty-five cents.

"Hurray!" shouted Crist. "Our first nugget!"

Bedrock was reached the next day, and several pans tested out from ten to thirty-five cents. We decided that a good three feet of pay dirt would average fifteen cents, and that a foot of bedrock would carry real pay, some of which we hoped would promise real riches.

A few days later the other shafts we had been sinking were down to bedrock and the results in each were much similar to those in the first. The news soon spread along the gulch that the boys on 39 had located "pay dirt," and our visitors were numerous. "Old Cummings" was among them. He inspected the gold we had panned, looked over the ground, the location of the shafts to the general lay of the gulch and gave us some much welcome advice as to further procedure.

"Here on this side of your claim, boys," he said, you have a high bench. It's deep, twenty-five feet to bedrock at least. Best leave that part and drift it out in the winter. Over there near the bed of the creek it can't be more than twelve feet and if you strip off the moss and ground sluice the muck you can cut down to eight feet. That will be easy for summer working.

To give us a head of water for sluicing, it would be necessary to construct a dam on the upper line of our claim, and for sluice boxes we would need lumber. We decided to go back down on Mammoth where the timber was good and saw out a lot of boards for the sluices, and also get logs for the dam.

We moved camp that afternoon about ten miles. Things were getting lively down below us. A hundred men were busy building cabins, sawing lumber, making boxes or prospecting their claims. For once Jim found plenty to do.

We built a sawpit and started sawing and cutting logs.

Sid Wilson came along with our outfits on his dog sleds. Crist went on up with him to our claim to see to the safe disposal of the things. On their return to where we were working, we engaged Wilson to haul up several loads of logs and lumber. It took about all the money we could rake and scrape up to pay him for this labor, but we felt that we were justified, having a sure prospect of pay in sight. It was well into April before we moved back to the claim.

Then there were the sluice boxes to be made, the dam to be built, and riffles to be got out for the sluice boxes. These latter were simply peeled spruce poles that would fit lengthwise in the sluice boxes, six of them lying side by side with a crosspiece nailed to top and bottom. They made crude but effective riffles for catching gold.

The dam was simply a crib work of logs filled with rocks, moss and earth, sunk into and across the bed of the stream. A crude and temporary affair it was, but we hoped it would suffice to raise the water high enough for our needs.

"There," said Jim one day. "Our boxes and riffles are ready, the dam is done,

From the Archives
of the
Circle District
Historical Society
Central, Alaska

Gold mining camp in spring.

moss cleared off the piece for summer working, now we are ready for business."

It was the first of May. The sun was getting high but still there was no sign of water rising in our creek as yet.

"Let's go hunting," suggested Crist. "I heard some men on Discovery got a caribou yesterday."

"Fresh meat would sure taste good, "said Kelley.

It was a two-hour climb up one of the "noses" to the elevated plateau from which rose Mastodon Dome, the central head of all the radiating creeks for twenty miles around us. This plateau, which we reached after a stiff climb, stretched out before us like a level, winding plain, with the dome swelling up from its center. Below us was our gulch, Mastodon. Independence and Miller Creeks lay on either side of it. Eagle, Wolf, and Unknown Creeks radiated on the other side. The plateau on which we stood was in some places a mile wide, in others contracted to a few rocks where streams from opposite sides converged, but we could see the mesa stretching away toward the northward for twenty miles to where Porcupine Dome, a twin to Mastodon, reared its head. But while we gazed entranced at the interesting scene, Kelley espied a herd of caribou approaching from near the head of Miller Creek.

A herd of caribou covering open ground.

"Down behind those rocks, boys," he whispered. "I believe they are headed straight towards us."

It was one of the advance group of caribou on their annual northward migration.

"Must be five hundred of them," said Kelley. "See them string along like a flock of sheep following a leader."

"Pick out a buck" said Jim. "They will be fatter than the does at this time of year."

"Looks as if they are all bucks," commented Crist, and so it proved. We learned later that generally the bucks were always in the lead of the big, annual movements, probably because they were stronger and more active than the females.

"Don't kill more than one or at the most two," I cautioned. "We couldn't use the meat and to kill more would be just murder."

Jim and Crist had guns and each selected a buck; when the herd passed within one hundred yards of our hiding place, each brought down his game. The herd, startled, broke into disorder, then after a few aimless bounds, one way and then another, huddled together and stood staring wonderingly at us. I am glad to write that in all my years in Alaska I was never guilty of reckless and criminal slaughtering of any wildlife. I wish I could write that all others had been equally so, but in those early days with no laws to curb a man, there was little thought given to the preservation of the then-abundant game, and some indulged in the sport of killing

90

wantonly. I heard of one man who boasted he shot one hundred caribou in one day.

As our caribou would dress out at about one hundred and twenty-five pounds each, we had all the meat the four of us could pack into camp. We realized that one animal would have been sufficient for our needs, but comforted ourselves with preparing to share some with our neighbors. The steaks and stews made an agreeable diversion in our regular line of meals. From that time on we were seldom without fresh meat. Generally a trip to the summit about once a week was made by some of us and we rarely returned empty-handed.

About a month after our first caribou hunt, Crist and I were up on the divide. The snow was fast disappearing and streams of water were trickling down into the gulches. While crossing a patch of snow, Crist suddenly stopped and pointed to a track crossing the snow.

"See there!" he exclaimed. "Isn't that bear track?"

It certainly was, and a fresh one too. We eagerly followed the track across the snow patch.

"Goes right into that pile of rocks," I said. "Perhaps the locality for a possible den or cave."

"Here it is!" shouted Crist. "The track leads right down under this ledge. There is kind of a hole or cave here."

A circular opening not much larger around than a barrel led under an overhanging boulder. The bear's track led to the mouth of the hole.

"The old lady is at home," said Crist. "Wonder if we can coax her out?" He tossed a small rock into the den and the response was immediate and startling. A rumbling roar and growl was followed by a scraping and scratching and the head and neck of an enraged bear protruded from the mouth of the den.

"Shoot, shoot!" shouted John. "She will be on us in a moment!"

We both fired point blank at the head and shoulders of the brute. In spite of the shock of two bullets at close range, the bear hurled herself out of the den and made a lurch toward us, only to be met by two more shots that finished her life. It was a full grown female. While examining our prize we heard a wheezing, snuffling sound from the den.

"Another bear!" exclaimed Crist, cocking his rifle and standing ready. The snuffling noise continued but nothing showed at the opening.

"Pitch in another rock, John," I suggested.

91

An Alaskan Adventure

Crist did so and we heard a growl and whine, but no bear showed itself.
"Must be a young one," I said. "Let's take a look and see if we can see anything."

By stepping down and peering under the rocks we could see into a sort of den or cavern, but it was too dark and indistinct to make out anything clearly.

"Need a light of some kind," said Crist.

Making a torch of a wisp of dried grass pulled off the rocks, we lighted it and dropped it into the den. The light flared up and we could plainly see not one, but two more bears huddled together and turning frightened eyes toward the blazing grass. Another wisp of grass was lighted and thrown down, and while it was blazing we shot and killed both bears. As soon as the smoke cleared, Crist crawled into the den and getting hold of a leg dragged the bears to the opening where I helped pull them out. They were very small cubs, and would not have survived without their mother. Crist and I hauled them back to camp, and got Kelley and Bullard to accompany us back to retrieve the large she-bear. We weren't too sure what we were going to do with three bears, but Old Cummings assured us that they would be splendid eating. He explained that bear meat in the spring, just when they were about to leave the den, was as sweet and tender as pork, and fat too, as the bears don't lose their full fat in the den, only after they come out and start to forage for food do they get lean and stringy. It was true and we never had such toothsome meals as those baked spare ribs from the cubs. Of course, we gave away the larger portion of the mother bear's meat, but Kelley tried out and saved some for cooking, and rendered out fifty pounds of lard. The skins too were in prime condition and we preserved them.

One other incident which occurred shortly after our bear hunt came near having a tragic ending. Jim and I had gone up on the divide one evening to kill a caribou. We had taken but one gun along and Jim was carrying that. Arriving on the summit, we paused to look around. It was getting along toward the middle of June and the days were now practically twenty-four hours long.

"I do believe, Jim," I said, "if we wait here till twelve o'clock we will see the sun rising around the horizon without setting. Over there toward the head of Miller Creek is a low divide and it's just about north from there too."

It was after eleven o'clock, so we sat down to await the interesting event. Slowly the sun, a great red disk, approached the horizon in a long, slanting line. Nearer and nearer it approached the earth.

"Ten minutes to twelve," announced Jim.

Five minutes more and the disc was still a clear space above the horizon line. "One minute to twelve, and just touching the line," continued Jim.

Another minute and the disc was clear and rising from the earth!

"Hurrah," I cried, "we have seen the midnight sun!"

While watching this interesting spectacle we had forgotten all about our errand. Now looking for game, we could see several herds of caribou scattered in different directions along the divide toward Miller Creek. One small bunch of about fifty was less than half a mile away.

"I believe, Jim," I said, "that I can go along behind this divide and run that bunch this way. If you hide behind this rock pile you can get one, then we won't have so far to pack the meat to camp."

The plan sounded feasible, so, keeping out of sight of the herd, I circled around them. Coming up suddenly behind them, I sprang out with a shout expecting to see the animals break and run, for like all deer tribe the caribou depend on their long legs to carry them out of danger. However, this bunch was composed of does with their young as well as a good sprinkling of bucks. Instead of breaking and running as I had expected, they ran, but ran toward me, and in a moment I was surrounded with a mass of excited and angry animals. The bucks kept getting closer and closer, stamping and striking with their forefeet. The does were trying to keep their young by their sides, and all were wildly milling around me. Nearer and nearer came the bucks, some were only twenty feet from me. I sorely regretted not bringing my gun! I picked up pieces of rock and hurled them at the bucks, hitting them severely. And just as things really looked pretty serious for me, the herd slowly began to run in a circle around me. Faster and faster they ran and I helped them by shouting and throwing rocks. At last they split, one portion going off toward the waiting Jim who presently bagged one, the other lot retreating in the opposite direction. Never again did I go hunting even such harmless creatures as caribou without a gun!

Chapter 16

We Cleanup Our First Gold

Summer, 1895

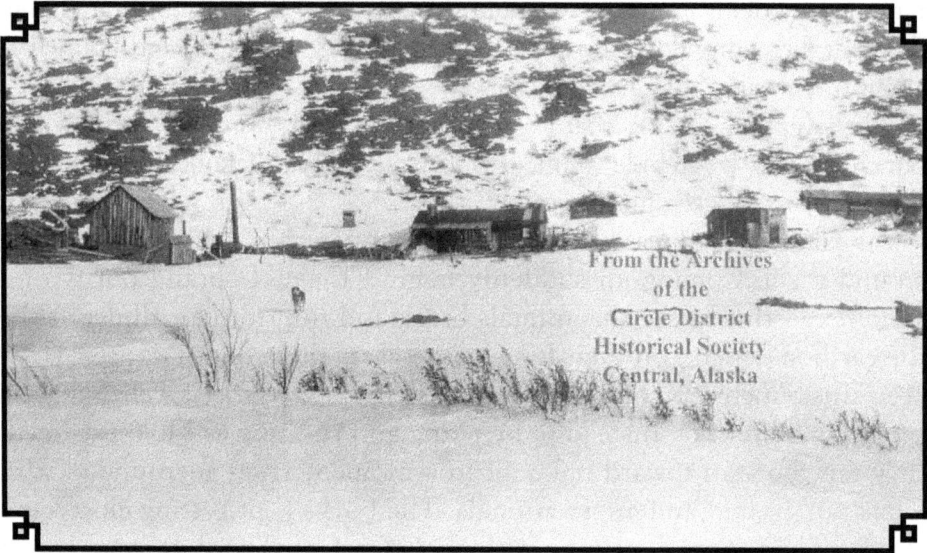

Dredge camp in spring.

By the fifteenth of June the snow was melting on the south side of the gulch and little streams were trickling down the sunny slopes, but it was not until a week later that a warm rain brought the long awaited ground sluice. That morning as Kelley opened the cabin door he was greeted by the sound of rushing water and he shouted for the rest of us to come out.

"The ground sluice is here, boys," he cried. "Rustle out!"

We piled out, seizing our shovels, breakfast forgotten for the moment. Our dam had filled and the water was pouring down our sluice-way over the stripped section that we had prepared for the summer's work. Our job was to train and direct the water so it would dissolve and carry away as much of the muck and lighter upper gravel, sand, and dirt as possible to reduce the amount of waste material overlying the pay dirt on bedrock.

All day we toiled, snatching only brief intervals for food, and by nightfall when the floodwaters showed signs of decreasing volume we had swept away at least four feet of the topsoil.

"Good," said Jim. "That leaves only about eight feet to shovel in and three or four feet of that should carry pay."

The next day the string of sluice boxes was set up on a line of eight, each twelve feet in length. Those sluice boxes, which we had made from the boards we had whipsawed down on Mammoth Creek, were twelve inches wide at one end, tapering to ten inches at the other so the smaller end of one box would just fit into the larger end of the one below, a tight joint being made by a strip of cloth where the ends lapped. Posts or logs about eight inches in diameter also supported the row of sluice boxes. Beginning at the lower box, the lower post was only three feet high; this was set upright and the first box placed on it and then braced on either side by a notched pole hooked over the side of the box and the other end held in place by a rock. A pitch or fall was given the sluice box of eight inches, thus each succeeding sluice box rose, higher and higher, as the last and upper one was reached. To establish a uniform grade we had made a "triangle" under the supervision of Old Cummings, our friend of long mining experience. The last thing to do before the boxes were ready for work was to install the set of riffles. These were the pole variety, simply peeled spruce poles about two inches in diameter, held together by cross-pieces nailed at each end of the set, the whole kept from washing out of the sluice box by a nail driven through the side of the box and into the crosspiece. This form of riffles was ideal for catching the coarse gold. The interstices between the pole riffles filled with small pieces of jagged rock which arrested the gold causing it to settle under the riffles.

When we had the boxes all up and braced, Jim commented, "Pretty high shoveling. About eight feet up to this last box. Of course, the string will be lowered as we work down, but the height will be the same."

"Well, it can't be helped," I replied. "Try turning in the water, Kelley, and we will see how it goes."

A stream of water that nearly filled the boxes was let in and all began shoveling the gravel and rocks into the sluice. The swift stream kept the material rolling and tumbling over the riffles and out at the other end, but after half an hour's work an ejaculation from Jim caused us to stop and look up.

"Gosh," he shouted, "just look at our tailrace, all chocked up!"

We had forgotten that someone had to tend the tailrace and keep the rocks and coarser material shoveled to one side or the whole works would soon be blocked up!

"One of us will have to put on his rubber boots and stay there at the tail all the time," I exclaimed. "I'll take the first time, and then we can take turns. That is the way they do it at Discovery, two hour shifts."

I found I had picked no sinecure and after two hours hard work in the icy cold water I was glad to shift jobs with Crist. As we were still several feet above pay dirt when we first commenced shoveling, we did not look for results from our first day's work, nor in fact for the next two, but on the fourth day when we shut off the water at noon the golden specks could be seen shining in the bottom of the boxes between the riffles! Three days and we were able to make our first "cleanup" under the supervision of Old Cummings, who had promised to initiate us into its mysteries. On the day appointed, we saw our old friend approaching, leisurely puffing on a short-stemmed black pipe. Seating himself on the woodpile he casually remarked that it was a fine day. Not heeding our manifest impatience and restlessness, he calmly continued to smoke his pipe and regaled us with the latest news. Pat Smith's ground had gone three ounces to the shovel (meaning a day's work per man); Henry Lewis was just making wages, while False Bottom Bill's claim did not pay out at all.

"How's yours lookin'?" he finally asked, getting up and strolling down toward the cut. "Fair, fair," he remarked meditatingly scrutinizing the bottom of the boxes. "Pretty good for a beginnin', do better when you get fairly at work."

He next directed us to take out the riffles from all but the last box. When this was done he turned in a small stream of water and gradually worked off the sand and fine rock that had lodged with the gold in the riffles. The lighter sand was rapidly crawling down the smooth bottom of the boxes, leaving the heavier gold. Pieces of flat rock placed here and there in the running water caused little eddies where the gold would accumulate. These little lots of metal Cummings took up with a flat tin scoop, and deposited in a gold pan. When the bulk of the gold had been secured in this manner, the last riffle was taken out and the contents under it, sand, gravel, and gold, caught in pans and then taken to the stream to be

From the Archives
of the
Circle District
Historical Society
Central, Alaska

Caribou herd crossing high country. Unidentified hunter in foreground.

washed. The gold was next dried in a pan on the stove and the remaining black sand carefully blown out. When through, the yellow metal filled one of our drinking cups half full. It looked dreadfully small and disappointing, but when weighed proved even better than Old Cummings had predicted. Forty-four ounces, or seven hundred and fifty dollars was in our cup!

"You've got good ground, boys," was Old Cummings verdict. "Two ounces and a half to the shovel is good enough. Now, don't kill yourselves with hard work, clean up pretty often, hold onto your dust and you can go outside and see your sweethearts in a couple of years with a well-filled poke."

After he was gone we could not help congratulating each other on our good fortune. We lifted and handled the golden grains, admiring the shape and beauty of successive pieces, weighing nuggets and selecting

Circle Hot Springs cabin and sled dog.

specimens for keepsakes. Though we had many subsequent cleanups as good or better than this one, none of them had the interest or romance attached to this first experience.

There followed a summer of hard work. We put in long hours for we knew that by the first of September the increased cold would shut off the running water and close down all sluicing for that year. Several claims above us were working and the whole six miles below us was a hive of industry. On Discovery, Pat and Jack had two shifts of twenty men working day and night. Now and then the tedium was broken by a call to a miners' meeting, usually on a Sunday. Those meetings were sometimes to pass regulations fixing boundaries of claims, sometimes to settle disputes between owners of claims and their employees. Almost always the decisions of the meetings were very fair and seldom disputed by the participants. We had nothing of the grim and memorable one in which Jacobi figured the previous winter.

One day in July we heard that Windy Jim had reached the gulch with supplies from the trading post. Bullard suggested I go down and see what he had and bring up what I could buy. We had had no butter, canned milk or many other "treats" for over two months. I was glad to go and went splashing down the soggy trail that went winding through the willows and niggerheads, crossing and re-crossing the stream as it zigzagged from one bank to the other. Acquaintances and friends hailed me as I passed their claims, inquiring as to our prospects and freely giving out their own. Little Doc had struck a rich pocket. Tom-the-Turk was doing well. Jimmie-the-Pirate had fair results, but thought his pay lay under a high bench and he expected to work that in the winter by drift mining.

At Discovery I found Windy Jim. His sobriquet had been fastened to describe his loose tongue. It was reported that at first he had strongly resented the title, but after a fistic argument with Handshaker Bob had gracefully accepted the name and even signed his signature in that manner at times. But Windy had sold all his stock when I arrived. He had packed in canned milk, butter and twenty-five pounds of fresh (one year-old) potatoes. The freight from Circle City of one dollar a pound that was added to the cost at the trading post boosted the price of these goods into the luxury class, but everything had gone like wildfire and Windy could have disposed of double the amount. I was just turning away disappointed after my useless trip when Jack Gregor hailed me from the door of his cabin.

"Hello, Fred," he called, "dinner just ready. Come on in and eat."

I did not need a second invitation, and oh, joy! There were boiled potatoes and butter, and milk from a can! Only those who have been deprived for months of these common everyday articles of food can realize how good those year-old potatoes tasted with real butter equally ancient. We certainly did justice to the meal and my only regret was that the other boys in my party could not have shared it with us.

Chapter 17
Stampede!

Circle Hot Springs.

One evening in July just as we were knocking off work for the day, George Kyler, whose claim was #40 just above us, came hurrying by.

"Big strike on the Porcupine," he called out. "All the Discovery men are off on a stampede and most of the men below here are going too. Better come along, Fred; I'm going to try to catch up with them."

An old-timer had once said to me, "When you hear of a strike, grab a can of sardines and a handful of hardtack and join the stampede. Put down a stake even if you have to climb a tree to do it. You never can tell where the gold is to be found."

I remembered his advice but forgot the sardines and crackers. Forgotten was supper and the hard day's work just over. I joined George a moment later.

"My idea," he said, "is that if we push up over the shoulder of the dome, drop down Wolf Draw, then up the nose on the other side we will hit the divide that leads to Porcupine and cut off at least ten miles that these other fellows will have to travel. You know that the divide makes a long swing around the head of Miller Creek."

A two-hour climb and we broke over the Mastodon shoulder and dropped down Wolf Draw, a six-mile tributary of Gold Run. There had been a stampede over there earlier in the season and I had a stake down myself somewhere along its course. No one was working that gulch the present summer, however, leaving its exploration for the coming winter season. We hurried and stumbled down the faint trail, mainly made by wild animals, bears and caribou or moose. It was getting pretty dusky when I bumped into George, who had suddenly stopped short.

"Hold on," he exclaimed, "there's a bear right ahead in the trail!"

Sure enough, there stood an old she-bear, erect on her haunches, weaving her head from side to side and uttering angry woof-woofs.

"An old she-bear with cubs," whispered George. "We don't want to monkey with her."

We had no guns with us anyway and as the old lady seemed determined to hold her ground, we edged off around her in the brush until well past her and her cubs.

"Lost a good ten minutes," grumbled George.

Two hours more and we breasted the nose leading to the Porcupine divide. We threw ourselves down on the ground to get a breathing spell after our strenuous exertions. Away off to the north, twelve or fifteen miles away, loomed Porcupine Dome, its snow-crowned head glowing in the midnight sun, which even on July 5 still shone on the snowy mantle.

Porcupine Dome, which gave birth to Preacher Creek, was as we knew being prospected by several parties that summer in search of the "Lost Preacher claim" which like so many lost claim stories was reported fabulously rich. It had been discovered, so the story went, by a preacher who on a hunting expedition picked up nuggets of gold on a tributary of that stream, hence the name. The preacher brought out the nuggets and showed them to a friend but could never relocate the place where he had found them. We had all heard the story, so when news came that there was a stampede onto Preacher Creek, we were very easily persuaded that the lost claim had been found. We eagerly turned our eyes along the divide in search of the stampeders from Discovery, but no person was in sight, neither along the divide toward Porcupine or back toward Miller and Mastodon.

"Can it be possible that they have gotten by here and out of sight already?" queried George.

"No, it can't be," I replied, "besides don't you see those bands of caribou standing there in bunches, sleeping as they do? They have not been disturbed or they would not be there now."

"That's so," answered George. "The stampeders never got along so far as here for sure. Let's go back around Miller and see if we can get any trace of them."

Back we started. All the excitement and fever of expectation had left us and now we were tired and hungry as well.

"Twelve miles from breakfast," groaned George.

Nothing was in sight as we plodded the weary miles back toward camp. However, we decided to drop down on Discovery and learn what had happened. Smoke was curling out of Chris Harrington's cabin as we drew near and the welcome smell of coffee and bacon filled the morning air.

"Hello, boys," called Chris. "Breakfast is just ready, come and eat."

"Where was the stampede, Chris?" we questioned as we sank on the camp stools and gulped down the steaming coffee.

Chris began to laugh as he asked, "Have you boys been on that fool stampede too?"

"What's it all about, Chris?" we demanded.

"Well, you see," he explained, "Tom-the-Turk, who works on the night shift, had been up the divide and shot a couple of caribou. He came back just as the day shift went to work and told some friends of his where part of the meat lay. They, like two fools, just dropped their shovels and without a word to anyone else started after the meat. The next man thought they had been tipped off on a new strike and he dropped his shovel and followed, and all the others struck out too. The first fellows, seeing a crowd coming and fearing they would lose their meat, broke into a run, and then of course we knew it was a big strike! So the excitement run all the way up the gulch, did it, clear up to 39 and 40. Oh well, you worked up a good appetite for breakfast anyway!"

That experience, strenuous as it was, did not cure me of stampeding and in less than a fortnight I was off again, but I did not forget the sardines and hardtack. And so passed the summer.

The first part of September saw the water getting low and ice formed in the sluice boxes. The sluicing was over. A council was held. Kelley decided that he would give up mining and go into partnership with a friend in the hardware business, chiefly making Yukon stoves. His share was equitably appraised and purchased by the three of us who decided to remain and drift mine our high bar.

"Much better than denning up in our cabin in Circle for six months as we did last winter," said Jim.

Chapter 18
I Make a Trip to Circle City

To drift mine we needed several things that would have to be obtained in the trading post. For the long, cold, dark winter we would need lights. Also, it was necessary to purchase our year's grubstake and have it freighted out to our claims.

"You go in, Fred," said Crist. "You stand well with Captain and Mrs. Healy and perhaps you can do better than anyone else in getting our outfit."

In those early days the question of an outfit for a year was the one important question. The price of an article was never mentioned or questioned. We gave the post trader our list of articles desired and he checked up what he could let us have. Usually the blue-pencil marks were the most prominent on the list. I remember one year when the influx of men had been greater than usual. Alex Younger had delayed his trip to the post rather late and his list got blue-penciled until nothing was left but a box of dried applies and two pick handles! I had been able to do some favors for the Healy's the previous year, and the boys felt that the Captain would do all he could for us.

While I would be gone, the other boys were to go down on Mammoth, cut logs for a cabin and whipsaw some needed lumber. Also, they would get a supply of firewood both for the cabin and for thawing the frozen ground. So far we had been living in a tent, but we all realized that a cabin was a necessity for winter.

It was a sharp, frosty morning when Kelley and I shouldered our light packs and started on the seventy mile trail to Circle City. Of the one hundred and fifty men who had worked on the gulch during the summer, fully two-thirds of them had already gone into the post. Their trail cut deep into the mossy tundra and was not easily lost, but was by no means easy to follow. Trodding knee-deep in the soft muck and moss or twisting and turning among the nig-gerheads, it was a hard day's tramp to do thirty miles with as light a pack as we carried. We were glad to stop for bed and supper at the Junction house where the trail forked, one branch going off on the right to Hoggum Gulch.

Another day brought us to the Indian village at Medicine Lake. Here we were just in time to witness a novel method of fishing practiced by these northern Indians. In the summer all the small Alaskan streams swarm with fish: trout, grayling, and salmon go up these watercourses to spawn. In the cold winters the small streams freeze solid. So the fish, by instinct, as soon as the ice begins to form, turn and run for the deep water of the Yukon and other large streams. The Indians would take advantage of this habit to lay in a stock of fresh fish for their winter supply. A fence of woven willow would be constructed and fastened across a riffle just below a deep pool. The fence would stop all the fish from a hundred miles above it. Soon the pool would be filled with a boiling, churning mass of crazy fish, eager to find a way to deep water.

Then the Indians would construct a platform of poles near the center of the fence. The upper end of the platform would rest on the ground in the shallow water. The other end ran a few inches out of the water and was held there by a couple of supports. The Indian women would range themselves on either side of the pole platform with their birch baskets handy. The fence would be cut at the platform and then the fun began. The fish would crowd and push and slide and slip along the platform where the women could gather them up and fill their baskets. Tons of fish were sometimes so gathered in the few days the fence stood, for if the ice formed and started to run, it quickly swept the fence away and released the imprisoned finny tribe. Such a harvest was in progress when we reached the village. The fresh fish were piled up on caches, where they quickly froze.

The third day brought us to the post and I bid Kelley good-by and good luck. The *P.B.Weare* steamboat had been in with supplies in July but those supplies were getting low. However, the *Weare* was sure to be back by October 1 and loaded with fresh goods from the outside.

My inquiry for lights brought out the fact that there were no candles for underground mining. Mrs. Healy had a pair of old-fashioned candle molds and some candle wicking. The Captain had some caribou tallow on hand and with this supply I had to be content for awhile, but the trader assured me the Weare should have some real mining candles when it arrived. But the Captain could let me have two small kerosene lamps and a case (two five gallon cans) of kerosene for our cabin. This case made a pack of 80 pounds a most unwieldy one. A hard wooden box of that weight with its swishy contents was worse than a 100 pound pack of flour!

I left liberal orders with Captain Healy for the rest of our outfit, and with our oil, tallow and a few odds and ends of little things returned to camp, leaving the heavier articles to be freighted out by Sid Wilson when the snow came.

That was a hard trip home. I remember how difficult it was packing that case of oil over the trail, and was glad to see Jim and Crist in their camp on Mammoth sawing lumber. Snow had fallen there already and we could use sleds getting our outfits up the gulch. A few weeks later, Wilson appeared with our outfits and his dogs were commandeered to haul our lumber and logs for our cabin to #39.

It did not take the three of us very long to put up and finish our winter home and to lay in firewood. This we got by going down the gulch two miles where the spruce thickets began. We had acquired a dog team by this time and Jim was especially proficient in getting the utmost work out of the willing malemutes.

"Now," said I, "let's lay in a good supply of meat to economize on bacon for the dogs, then we will be ready for winter."

The southern migration of the caribou had begun and countless herds of fifty to five thousand were crossing the head of our gulch daily. They were hog fat too at this time of the year. We made a trip to their runway and killed several each day. Many more could have been slaughtered, but we only killed what we could take care of each day. A night on the woodpile and the meat was frozen solid. This frozen meat was then packed in our cache which, by the way, was a small covered cabin of logs built on high posts for safety from the wolves. We did not cease our "marketing" as Crist termed it until twenty-five caribou were safely stored away. Our meat supply for the winter was assured.

Chapter 19
Drift Mining
Winter, 1895

Winter drift mining was an innovation, and it was soon adopted by the miners as much to break up the long months of inactivity as in the hopes of any material gain. There were many gulches where the depth of frozen soil was so great that there was no possibility of the sun thawing the ground to bedrock, and in nearly every gulch as in Mastodon where we were working, there were numerous high bars that were equally impossible to work from the surface. It was one of these bars that we proposed to tackle this winter.

The procedure at first was similar to the prospecting we had done the previous year. First, a six-by-eight shaft had to be thawed by means of wood fires to bedrock, thirty feet below the surface. That took a month. Lots of wood and plenty of hand work was required. It kept one man and the dog team steadily at work hauling the wood.

As the shaft deepened we had to rig up a windlass and bucket for hoisting the thawed ground. That was Crist's job. He was a carpenter by trade and had a good set of tools. In fact, so neat a job of both bucket and windlass was turned out that he was in demand by neighboring mine owners to make a set for them, and quite a bit of ready dust flowed into our treasury as we always helped him with the project.

By the first of November our shaft reached bedrock, and our pannings showed that three feet of gravel and almost one foot of bedrock carried pay about equal to the ground we had worked in the summer. Crist had made a mud box to hold the water for our test pannings. We had to melt snow for water both for our own use and for panning. The mud box was kept in a corner of the cabin and Jim spent an hour or more every evening testing our gravel, a sample of which he brought up with him from the shaft.

As soon as our shaft was down to bedrock and we had all determined we were on a body of pay dirt, the procedure was somewhat different from that followed in sinking the shaft. A much smaller fire was laid, and great care was taken in the manner of placing it or else the heat would melt and cave off a great deal of waste material, all of which would have to be hoisted out of the shaft and thrown away.

A method of burning underground was illustrated to us by our friend Cummings. First, a mass of dry kindling and dry sticks was piled against the bank to be thawed. In this case, it meant all around the base of the shaft. Next, all these dry kindlings were covered by a compact layer of green logs sloping over the kindlings from the floor of the shaft up about two and a half feet against the side of the wall. Sometimes the green logs themselves were also covered with a layer of moss which we could cut out in great slabs a foot thick in almost any part of the gulch. The fires were started in several places in the dry material and smoldered and burned slowly much like a charcoal burner's fires. The idea was to confine the heat as much as possible to the bottom and side of the shaft and let as little heat as possible escape through the roof above the burning wood.

In the morning the fires would have burned out, the waste material they had thawed out and dropped down on the screen of green logs was shoveled off, hoisted and dumped to one side. Then the logs and any unburned pieces of wood were removed and carefully laid aside for the next fire. The thawed pay dirt was the next and the most important order of business. If the fire had done good work, we generally found a foot of the wall was ready to hoist out. This, of course, contained pay material and was carefully piled out away from the waste material. It was from this pay dirt that Jim made his evening pannings. A careful account was kept of the results in a little book Jim hung up on a nail near his bunk. As the work progressed and the diameter of the underground workings increased, pannings had to be taken from several points to see that we were not thawing out worthless ground. As the days and weeks rolled along, our pile of pay dirt grew to be a mound, then to quite a hill.

A little before Christmas, 1895, Jim announced that according to his records of pans and quantity of dirt taken out, our pay hill contained fifteen hundred dollars more or less. All this, of course, and the remainder of the dirt taken out during the winter would have to be sluiced in the spring, but it could be quite quickly handled then from the loose heap on top of the ground.

Although Jim spent a good share of his evenings panning in the cold, wet mud box, he was not the only one who had a busy time. Crist, who disliked cooking, but delegated that job to me while he got up the wood and melted the snow for water. I had a generous sourdough box hanging from the roof of the cabin over the stove. In this I had a batter that had been working all day. The first thing I did in coming in from work was to take down the box, stir

Circle Hot Springs and log pile (firewood).

in enough flour to make a stiff dough which I worked into loaves, placed in tins and set on a shelf just behind the stovepipe. Here the loaves raised while I prepared supper and did the housework. About an hour before bedtime, the loaves were ready for the oven. They baked while we prepared for bed and we had bread ready for the next day. In making the bread, a little of the "starter" was left in the bread box, this was the mere addition of warm water and more flour was beat into a thin batter, and the box was hung over the stove again. By next morning there was a box full and sometimes overflowing of a most appetizing pancake batter. These hot cakes, bacon and coffee constituted our breakfast. A pot of beans was kept bubbling on the stove at all times, and a caribou roast was usually in order for our other meals. The cold weather and our hard work gave us great appetites and it was well we had laid in such a good supply of fresh meat.

A little incident comes to mind at this time. When I was at the post in the fall, I had ordered our outfit and arranged to have it freighted out by Sid Wilson. When we were looking over the articles, we had discovered a box that read "Evaporated Potatoes from Santa Clara, California." I recalled that Mrs. Healy had told me they were expecting some of the new dehydrated vegetables and we agreed this must be one of them. I decided to treat the boys one day and we opened up the box. The potatoes, sliced about the size and thickness of poker chips, and glistening white, filled the twenty-five pound box which had cost us twenty-five dollars.

"Looks good," commented Jim, trying to bite into one. "Hard though. Have to be cooked I guess."

"Here's the directions," said Crist. "Soak in cold water and boil until tender, season to taste."

"Well, here is plenty of cold water, let's have some for dinner," I said.

We got a bucket and clawed out about a quart of the slices which were then covered with cold ice water.

"Now," said Crist, "Jim and I have work out at the shaft. You look after the things, Fred, and we'll have a potato feed for dinner."
I looked at the lot several times during the morning but could not see that the cold water had made any impressions upon them. However, about noon I put the bucket on the stove with a good fire under it and soon had them bubbling at a great rate. Before long the boys came stomping in.

"Hello!" cried Jim. "How are the Irish? Ready to eat?"

"Sorry, boys. I've had them boiling for half an hour but they don't seem to be getting soft yet."

"Here, let me see 'em," said Crist.

Getting a fork he tried to spear or prick one, but it only slid away from him. Finally, by a dexterous flip, he popped a piece out of the kettle onto the floor. A moment later after picking it up he examined it.

"Just as hard as it was this morning!" he declared. "The boiling hasn't fazed it a particle!"

"Too bad, boys," I said, "but here are beans and a nice caribou stew. I'll keep the potatoes boiling this afternoon and they surely will be ready for supper."

As a matter of fact, although I kept the fire going all that afternoon and evening, the potatoes never did cook soft! Even the dogs, who never turned down things in the eatable line, all refused to have anything to do with the mess! One evening sometime later I saw Jim go to the box, select half a dozen slices and then with an awl drill holes in the slices.

"What in the world are you doing, Jim?" I inquired.

"I'm turning these blasted poker chips into pants' buttons," he explained. "Might as well get some good out of them and I am short on pants' buttons."

Chapter 20
Christmas Potlatch

A few days before Christmas, Crist said to me, "Fred, I wish you would take the dogs and chase yourself down to the post and see if you can't manage to get some little things. We are out of butter, milk is most gone, and we will need another box of candles before long. What say?"

"It's fine with me," I replied. "It's sharp, nippy weather, but the dogs feel fine. It will take two days to go in, three out, one day in the post, six days. I'll be back Christmas day."

The dogs were wild to go and early in the morning in the cold, frosty starlight we started. It was all downgrade past Discovery and through the thick timber of Mammoth where we had cut our lumber. After a long afternoon following the trail down Crooked Creek, crossing and re-crossing to cut off bends, I pulled up at Windy Jim's roadhouse, half way to the post.

The first thing on a trip like this was to see that the dogs were fed and cared for. That always came before one's own needs. A dried salmon to the dog is a meal per day, always given at night. If the salmon cannot be obtained, the driver has to cook a mess of flour and bacon, which takes time and was much more expensive than fish. Fortunately, when we got the dogs in the fall from some Indians, we also got a liberal supply of dried fish, so I lost no time in giving the dogs their supper. At camp we did not bother with sleeping quarters for the dogs, as they much prefer to burrow in the snow as did their wolfish ancestors, but here at a roadhouse where there was a likelihood of several teams meeting and dog fights resulting, Windy had provided separate pens in another log building. Popping the dogs into one of these pens, I sought the roadhouse where I found a rousing fire of birch logs and a warm supper steaming on the rude table.

Here I met several former acquaintances. There were two freighters going up to the mines with loads, a couple of men from Hoggum going into the post, and there was Jimmy Funchion who said he was doing a little trapping, picking up some nice marten skins and he had taken several foxes, one of them with a silver tip.

There were wooden bunks along the walls into which we rolled our own bedding and for which crude sleeping accommodations Windy Jim charged one dollar. Meals were likewise at the same price.

I made an early start the next morning, then pushed across the ten mile tundra to the trading post and the lights of Circle City shown twinkling through the late evening dusk. I spent a very pleasant evening sitting around the fire with Captain and Mrs. Healy listening to news of the camps, the doings at the post and seeing copies of the late papers (only six months old.) Luckily for us, the Captain could let me have a box of candles, some butter and milk and would even make up a mixed case of canned goods. It seems Mrs. Healy had had a similar experience in cooking and they had given up the new food as a failure. I might mention right there that the next year the manufacturers of the dehydrated products cooked the potatoes first, then the dehydrated and pulverized results formed a very desirable addition to our food.

I made a quick run the next day up to our old cabin in the spruce thicket above town. It stood snow-covered and deserted, as were all the other cabins except one from which smoke was coming. I knocked at the door and found Frank Montgomery and Jerry Heater having a game of cards. They gave me a cordial handshake, inquired about Jim and Crist and extended an invitation for dinner. Frank and Jerry were going prospecting over on South Birch Creek as soon as the short days passed. They would go out by way of Hoggum and cross the divide at the pass.

"It's big country there," commented Frank. "It's never been looked over."

"Well, good luck, boys," I said. "Hope you strike it rich."

On the return trip with a light load, but a most precious one as Mrs. Healy had added several little additions to the Captain's supplies, I remembered the fishing incident I had witnessed on the previous fall at Medicine Lake. Reaching the point where the trail branched to the Indian village, I turned off and a short half mile brought me to Albert's cabin. Albert's wife, whom we called Maggie, had been at school at the Nulato Mission so could speak English fairly well. It was just midday when I arrived and the family were about to eat. They had a pot of meat stewing and Maggie's two children were chewing on pieces of dried salmon. There was no bread, of course. Albert motioned for me to join them, and I added to the meal by bringing in a sack of pilot bread or hardtack, some sugar and black tea. How the children's eyes glistened at the sight of the treats, and Maggie too showed she knew how to use the hardtack and promptly broke up several of the cakes into the stew. Tea, very sweet, was also a rare luxury to the Indians, and the old people, Maggie's parents, smacked their lips over the cups I poured out for them.

It was a most enjoyable meal but the dessert capped the climax.
I saw Maggie whisper to Tatsu, her twelve year old daughter. Tatsu took a birch bark basket and went out into the woods and presently returned with a basket full of clean, white snow. While she was gone, Maggie had taken a kettle in which she placed some bear's fat. This she gently heated over the fire until the fat was melted, then taking handfuls of snow she stirred it into the fat, repeating the process until she had a creamy white mass not unlike ice cream in appearance. This dessert she dished out in birch bark plates. Being short of spoons when she came to me she took the spoon out of the stew kettle and licked it clean! As we ate our "cream", Albert turned to me and grunted, "Hi you skakum muck-u-muck?" I agreed with him that it was very good!

Remembering that Maggie had been to a Mission school and that the day after tomorrow was Christmas day, I told her that I had a "Klootchmun" (wife) outside and little ones like her Tatsu and Pitka, and that on Christmas their mother would give the little ones potlatch, their word for presents. I illustrated it by giving each of the children some lumps of sugar, repeating

"Christmas potlatch." To Maggie I gave a bright red handkerchief, to Albert some tobacco, and to the old father and mother some tea with sugar to sweeten it, repeating the Christmas potlatch each time.

Then I bartered with Albert for a lot of the frozen fish and a quarter of a moose that he had killed shortly before. I was ready to start on the home trail when Maggie came out of the cabin, climbed up the ladder to their cache and came down with a piece of meat, the hindquarters of some animal.

Handing it to me she quaintly said, "Christmas potlatch!"

"What is it, Maggie?" I asked as I did not recognize the kind of meat it was. "Is it caribou? No, it's too small for that."

"Oh," she said, "cat."

"Wild cat!" I ejaculated. "Oh no, Maggie. Indian eat cat. White man no eat cat," and I started to hand the carcass back to her.

"No, no," she said refusing to take back the present. "Heap good. All same rabbit. Christmas potlatch!"

So, realizing that she had given it to me in the spirit of Christmas goodwill, and because I had given to her and her children, I gravely thanked her and placed the cat on my load thinking to give it to the dogs for their supper. Later on, remembering Maggie had said, "Heap good. All same rabbit," I thought, "Why not? I'll try it on Jim and Crist!"

Another night at the Junction and Windy Jim's, the next at the sawpit on Mammoth, and I reached home at noon on Christmas day. We were all glad to get home, dogs and myself, although I had enjoyed the trip hugely. The boys, too, were glad to see me back.

"What did you get, Fred?" eagerly inquired Crist.

"Oh, candles, and milk and butter, and fixings from Mrs. Healy, and a load of fish from the Indians, and look there—a quarter of moose meat."
I did not mention the cat which I had taken pains to wrap up in my bedding so the boys would not see it.

"We'll have a fine dinner tonight, boys," I said, "and I'll cook it."

"Good," said Crist. "Come on, Jim, let's finish getting out that thaw and lay the fires in the shaft for the night."

When they were gone, I got out the potlatch present and looked at it. It was white and fat and surely did look "heap good." Getting it into a pan and making a stuffing of crumbled bread mixed in milk, butter, salt, pepper, and some sage Mrs. Healy had given me, I popped it into the oven and before long a savory sage odor pervaded the cabin.

Coming in an hour later for an errand, Crist sniffed the odor stopped short and exclaimed, "By George, that smells like turkey! What is it?"

"Never mind," I replied. "You know I told you Mrs. Healy gave me some fixings."

Crist went out and I heard him calling down to Jim that "Fred had a turkey for dinner!"

I had the table all set when the boys came in. I had opened a can of peaches, there was real butter on a plate, coffee was bubbling on the stove, and the "turkey", nicely browning in the oven, was sending out most appetizing smells.

"Sit down, boys," I directed. "Everything is about ready. Jim, you carve the turkey. Help yourselves to dressing, plenty of it."

"Come on yourself. What are you waiting for!" inquired Crist.

"I'll be there in a minute, just as soon as I get these loaves in the pan so they will start raising. Don't wait for me," I replied.

"Say, Jim, this tastes good," said Crist, taking a liberal helping of the turkey.

"Sure does," replied Jim. "Come and eat, Fred."

"But what in thunder is it?" suddenly asked Crist as he cut out the leg bone. "Never saw anything like it! This isn't a turkey bone!"
Jim turned to me and demanded, "What is it and where did you get it?"

"Oh," I responded." "Cat. Heap good. All same rabbit!"

Chapter 21

We Sell Our Claim

1896

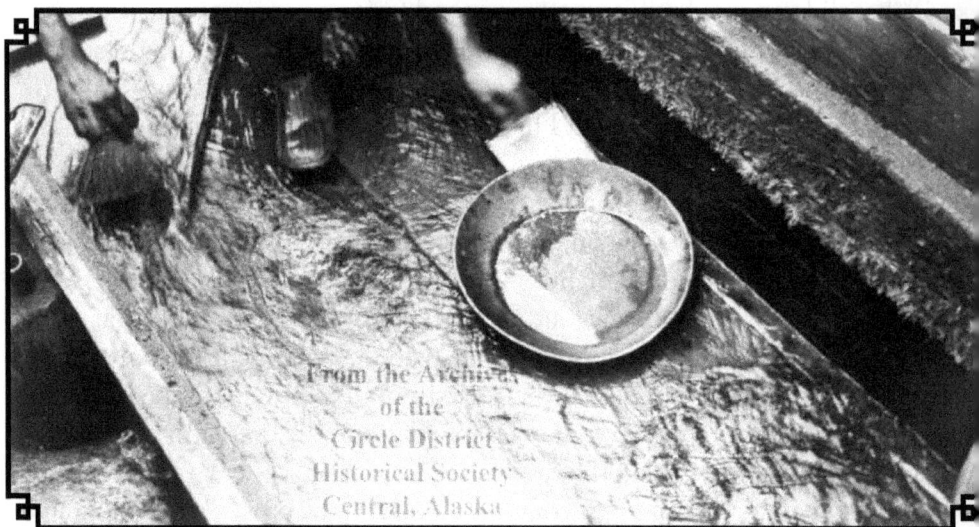

Cleaning up a sluicebox

And so the winter passed. We did hard work, had many pleasant experiences, spent wonderful nights looking at the northern lights which were magnificent. We were a congenial crowd, never wrangled as marred some of the camps. Occasionally a joke was played on each other as when I palmed off cat on the boys for turkey, but wholly pleasant memory of all the year remained to all of us.

With the spring run of water, we first sluiced our winter dump of pay dirt with the returns coming very close to Jim's calculations, showing how careful he had been in keeping his records.

The spring influx of new men, both by trail and later up the river by steamboat, brought us letters from home and papers. Nearly two years had lapsed since I had heard from home, and the latest letters received were still three months old. One batch of letters coming in over the Chilkoot Pass had been lost in the canyon and the carrier of them drowned. Of course, my family had been greatly surprised at my change of plans, but Abbie's last letter told of getting some of mine, written at Forty Mile, so she knew I had arrived safely at my destination. Now that the government had established a mail route both overland and by water, we could reasonably expect to get mail no more than three months old at the latest.

After the spring cleanup we turned to the open cut again where we had worked the previous summer. We even hired some additional help for now there was a surplus of new men. Ten dollars a day was the regular wages we paid.

Late in the summer we received an attractive offer for our property, and talking it over we decided to accept it. Jim would go to work for Pat and Jack on Discovery. Crist would help Captain Healy put up some new buildings and I decided to go outside, but intended returning. (Indeed, I had a plan in mind that I had long kept in the back of my head.) The new purchaser of the claim would take over any surplus outfit, in fact he bought everything but our personal belongings that we might wish to carry with us. So, on a frosty September morning, Crist and I shouldered our packs, and with our gold dust strapped to our dogs we turned our faces toward the post and for me, home.

Nothing of importance occurred on the way out except at the junction of Crooked Creek and Birch Creek one of the dogs loaded with our gold just fell, or jumped, into the water and, of course, went to the bottom at once. We nearly lost him in the current, but fortunately fished him out just in time. Of course, the dust was not injured.

At the post I found the old S.S. *Arctic* just unloading and would pull out for St. Michael the next day. There was just time for a hasty good-by to friends in the post, and we were off on the six day run down the river to the ocean port of St. Michael.

Although the Yukon is a mighty river, by September the water is getting low on the bars and navigation is difficult. Twice we stuck on shoals, but worked off by cable and winches. The river at the mouth splits into many channels and these lead out in twisting, tortuous ways far into the Bering Sea. It is not unusual for even one of these flat bottomed riverboats to stick on a mud flat out in the sea ten miles off from land. Captain Mayo, however, knew his way and safely round Point Romanzof and brought the boat into St. Michael's harbor where the ocean ships discharge their cargo.

There were no regular boats on which transportation could be secured, but I found a tramp barkentine of three hundred tons just unloaded. The captain, for a consideration of $80 each, was willing to take us out if we would agree to bunk in the hold on a load of canned salmon he was under contract to pick up at Kodiak Island. We agreed (about seventy of us) and set sail for Dutch Harbor and Unimak Pass which lets out into the Pacific Ocean. We had scarcely gotten out of sight of land when a regular Bering northwester set in and howled for three days! Then followed fog and storm. We did not see the sun for two weeks. The captain was completely "at sea" (literally) as to our position. It was nine hundred miles to Unimak Pass, but how far we had drifted off our course he could not tell. In a lull of the storm, the United States cruiser, *Bear*, loomed up and gave us our reckoning.

But now a new danger confronted us. Expecting to load at Kodiak, the captain had only provisioned for ten days and we were short of food already. However, we were on a cod bank and all hands were set to work hauling in cod, for in a pinch one can live on fish alone!

Then another two weeks of storm and fog enshrouded us and we still had not reached the pass. The morning of the thirty-fifth day I went on deck. It was glorious, bright and clear, with a wind bowling us along toward the northeast.

"Boy," said the captain rubbing his hands briskly, "we will be in Kodiak with this wind by tomorrow night."

I silently pointed to Mt. Shishaldin smoking over on our starboard side.

"Looks to me, Captain, you are on the wrong side of that smoker."

You never heard such profanity as poured from the mouth of that man! He was on the wrong side and running up Bristol Bay. We had never got out of the pass at all! The orders flew thick and fast, and we had to spend a whole day beating back to the desired opening. This was made the next morning.

The miners aboard then called a meeting and the captain was informed that owing to the long delay he must give up his plan to stop at Kodiak, and that we insisted on a direct course for Seattle or San Francisco. The captain stormed and swore he would not do it, that it was mutiny on the high seas! But seventy determined men, many of them miners and prospectors, only laughed at him. His crew of six men were more than ready to side with us for they too had been on starvation rations. So sail was set for Seattle and six days later, forty-two days from St. Michael, we dropped anchor at Port Townsend and our party separated for our various destinations. Mine was first San Francisco, and the mint where my dust was converted into coin of the realm, then home overland to Wisconsin to wife and children.

Kodiak Island and the Aleutian Chain

Chapter 22
A Year at Home, River Falls
1897

If I am ever to complete this narrative, this year at home must be passed over in a few lines. First, a new house must be built. We purchased an acre of land adjoining the school grounds, and a seven room house with modern furnishings was erected. My two and a half years in Alaska had produced enough revenue to provide for this home. Into this we moved, and Abbie's mother, now a widow, came to live with us too.

During all this time, I was carrying out those plans I mentioned previously that I had contemplated while mining on Mastodon. The Forty Mile River, Seventy Mile River, and Birch Creek were all gold streams running into the Yukon that began in the mountains lying between the Yukon and Tanana River. My idea was that streams flowing from those mountains into the Tanana must also be gold bearing, and that to prospect them one should get into Tanana country. Indians from that section coming over onto the Yukon to trade had brought both gold and copper nuggets. So, my big idea was to build a small steamboat and, with a few companions, go up the Tanana on a prospecting trip, using the steamboat to carry two or three years' supplies.

Meanwhile, the discovery of gold on the Klondike had electrified the world, and an unprecedented rush to those fields was taking place. Thousands of men and women poured over Chilkoot Pass and the equally impassible White Pass by way of Skagway. Hundreds lost their lives through accident, exposure or disease.

I had given several "talks" in home town and cities featuring Alaska and conditions there. I was visited several times by delegations of interested parties and had more than one opportunity to guide expeditions into that northern country. I declined them all because my plans for an independent outfit were maturing. Four young men had been selected as companions. They were Ed Conrad of Hammond, Wisconsin, Tom Brown, Oliver Torrance, and Charles Bliss of Minneapolis. Conrad and Bliss were married, Bliss' wife was a second cousin of mine. Brown and Torrance were single men. Each one of us five contributed one thousand dollars toward the expense of the expedition. We let a contract to a Racine, Wisconsin boat builder for the construction of a forty foot sternwheel boat with a fifty horse power marine boiler. When loaded, she would carry five tons of provisions and be suitable for ascending the Tanana and its tributaries. This boat was shipped over the Northern Pacific Railroad to Seattle, and arrangements were made with one of the steamboat companies for transportation to the mouth of the Yukon River.

Perhaps a few words as to the personnel of our party would be in order at this point in my narrative. Ed Conrad, from Hammond, a small town near our own home place, was of German descent. An all around handyman, he could mend a broken watch spring, sharpen a pick or make a batch of bread. If a table were to be constructed, a door to be hung, or a cabin to be build, Ed was there "with both feet" as Tom expressed it. Tom Brown was Scotch, a city boy, but strong, willing and capable. There was not a lazy bone in his body. We soon all appreciated his helpful hands. Oliver Torrance, "Ollie", as we called him, was a regular "Micky" and had all the original wit and repartee of the Irish. He was the life of the party, although as far as that goes we all were a cheerful bunch. Charles Bliss, whose business was insurance broker-age, was an Eastern man originally from Hartford, Connecticut. He was most methodical and careful in his ways. He was always willing to learn whenever the work and experiences were new to him, and he never shirked, attacking anything no matter how disagreeable it might be. Of course, my previous experience in the North was considered an asset by the party.

Chapter 23

Experiences With Our Steamboat
1898

One more Christmas at home and in the early spring of 1898 we all bid good-by to our families and friends and set off for Seattle, where we spent several weeks purchasing our outfit and getting everything ready for a three-year sojourn in the northern land. In Seattle, we met one of the groups that had been to visit me the previous winter in River Falls. They too had a steamboat which they had christened *Tanana Chief*, and learning of our destination they asked to join in with my party for mutual help and companionship. We were glad to do so and later developments proved the wisdom of so doing.

One rather amusing incident occurred while we were waiting in Seattle. One morning the call boy at the hotel came paging "Captain Currier." Thinking possibly I was the one wanted, I made myself known and I was informed that the captain from the sailing ship S.S. from Boston by ways of Cape Horn was seeking me.

"Captain," he explained, "I learned you have been in Alaska. I wish you would come aboard the S.S. and see a party of 'school marms', sixty of them, that I have aboard."

"But, Captain R.," I replied, "what have I to do with a school marm, let alone sixty of them!"

"Well, just come aboard if you will," he begged. "I am at my wit's end to know what to do with the lot!"

Accordingly, I accompanied him to the wharf and stepped into his waiting boat where two sailors with grins on their faces took up the oars and rowed out to the low lying, black hulled ship riding at anchor. On the way out, the captain explained his predicament to me. It seems this party of Boston school teachers had purchased some claims in the Klondike district, formed an association to mine them, and with their outfit had contracted to be taken to St. Michael, making the long trip by way of Cape Horn. The three months stormy ocean voyage had disheartened more than half of the party, and dissatisfaction with the management had brought about dissensions and recriminations among them. The party was contemplating breaking up and disbanding at Seattle.

119

I was introduced to Miss M., the leader, and she invited me to attend a meeting in the large dining room, the only feasible gathering place on the ship. I listened to their plans, was told of the wildcat claims they had purchased, ran over a check of the supplies they owned etc. I noted a ton of "barbed wire fencing."

"My dear Miss M., what is the idea of the 'barbed wire'?" I inquired.

"Why," she innocently explained. "I understand that there are many rough and unscrupulous men in the mines and I want to fence our claims to protect ourselves from them."

This was only a sample of the wild, irrational plans and outfits of so many of the parties outfitting that spring! I could only point out to those ladies the hardships and dangers ahead of them, and that the wildcat claims they had purchased were in all likelihood worthless. I explained that known good claims did not have to be hawked about the country in search of purchasers. I learned later that the party did disband, most of the members returning to the East to take up their professions again.

The school marm party was only one of over seventy outfits that were formed that year. Some, in fact most of them, went to pieces at St. Michael. A very few of the groups went on to penetrate the interior. I remember meeting a party of sixty New Englanders who called themselves the Vermont Party. They had reached St. Michael and were engaged in putting together two boats they had shipped in a knockdown condition. In the party were doctors, lawyers, ministers, bank clerks, farmers and even an undertaker. Two years later I met one of them on the Tanana River.

"Hello, Vermont," I greeted him. "How's the party?"

"I am it," he replied. "All the rest are dead, drowned, or gone back home!" That laconic epitaph could have been written on 90% of all those quixotic Eldorado dreams.

By April, 1898, our party of five were aboard a ship and en route for the Bering Sea. A week of not unpleasant voyage and we dropped anchor at Unalaska, near Dutch Harbor in the Aleutian Islands. The Unimak Pass that had so baffled us on the trip out in the fall of 1896 offered no difficulty this time. I told the boys of our many days' search for the outlet in the sailing vessel.

"It's just like a trap," commented Tom, "Lets you in all right, but won't let you out again."

At Unalaska, the U.S. cruiser *Bear* informed us that ice still covered the Bering Sea and it would probably be six more weeks before passage to St. Michael would be clear. The ship's management decided to unload its passengers and cargo at Unalaska, return to Seattle for another consignment and pick us up later. This plan caused great dissatisfaction, but nothing could be done about it. We were promptly unloaded and our outfits dumped on the shore. We busied ourselves in getting up a tent and housing our goods. Our boat, shipped intact, was towed into a sheltered cover and tied up safely. The Tanana party had a larger boat and it was knocked down for transportation. The men in this group now decided to put it together on the shores at Unalaska and have it towed across to its destination. We all turned to help them and aided them in the work, glad to be relieved of the tedium of the long wait on the island. We completed the Tanana boys' boat, and also we put together our own scow that we had ordered as an aid in carrying cargo up the river. After these jobs were done, we did a little sightseeing. We made a visit to the Greek church at Dutch Harbor, and occasionally called at the Jessie Lee Home for orphaned girls in Unalaska. The weather was getting pretty rugged, with the "woolies", terrific winds, sweeping down upon us out of the icy north.

At last the steamer returned and picked us up. Our boat and scow were loaded on deck, but the *Tanana Chief* was too large for that and had to be towed behind the steamer. Sid Wariner and Bill Osone, two of the Tanana party, elected to ride on the Chief. It was a rather perilous trip if a storm should arise while crossing the nine hundred miles to St. Michael. However, the trip was uneventful and we arrived safely at our destination. My contract called for unloading at the mouth of the Yukon River. St. Michael was eighty miles distant up the coast and I had realized that the eighty miles represented a dangerous stretch for our small flat bottomed craft. The steamship company objected to unloading us at the mouth of the river as all the other outfits, except the *Tanana Chief*, had been billed to St. Michael, and it involved considerable extra expense to move our small equipment to the Yukon's mouth as well as some danger to their larger boats. Two good friends came to my rescue just as it seemed I was about to lose my case. Two inspectors of hulls and boilers refused to give the A.C. Company clearance papers on its riverboats unless the company complied with its contract to me and the Chief boys.

St. Michael's Bay was alive with shipping as our boat, the *Governor Pingree*, swung out in a long, graceful curve past Egg Island and took her course directly out to sea in order to reach the channel between Stewart and St. Michael's islands. From here we headed directly for Point Romanzof, distant thirty-two miles on a south-easterly direction. Pastolik Bay, immediately beyond, was the dread of all the steamboat men plying between the Yukon River and the ocean port of St. Michael. Here it was said a person could wade for fifty miles out to sea without getting beyond his depth. The *Pingree* drew but three feet of water, but half a dozen times we were aground and the prospect of reaching the mouth of the river looked dubious, especially as the breeze began to freshen and an ominous ground swell came in from the ocean. For two hours the captain swept the distant shore with his glasses before he discovered the Eskimo pilot we were expecting. He came paddling out in his skin bidarka and readily agreed to guide us into the Yukon mouth for the moderate sum of six dollars. In and out and back and forth he took us, each time bringing us nearer the shore until at last he announced, "Yukon mouth" and demanded his money.

A couple of low, swampy islands, their grass-covered surface just above the water, were all there were to indicate land, but pointing to the narrow ribbon-like opening between them, which led away southward, our pilot assured us that this was the Aphoon mouth and our course lay in that direction. Our contracts called for the delivery of our freight within the mouth of the river. I had remembered Kotlik, a small Indian village, about five miles up the river as a desirable spot to disembark, but unfortunately, when a mile below that place, the *Governor Pingree* ran hard and fast on a sandbar and it was decided to unload our freight on a low grassy bank close by. The place was swampy and bred myriads of mosquitoes, but as those pests were everywhere we knew we had to submit to the inevitable. Two days were spent in unloading freight and four more in putting the finishing touches to our boat and getting ready to start up the river.

I can do no better than to quote from a letter written home describing our trip up the river on our own boat which we had christened *Potlatch*.

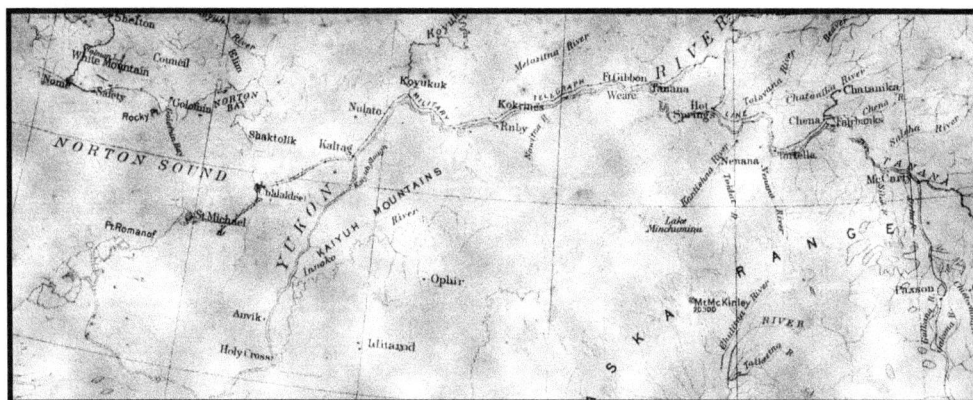

Western Interi

Potlatch and Tanana Chief with barges on Tanana River

On board the steamer *Potlatch*
August 20, 1898

Dear Folks:

When I wrote you last we were on the point of leaving St. Michael for the mouth of the Yukon River, there to begin the long river trip for ourselves. I believe I mentioned that the party, twelve in number, who owned the *Tanana Chief* were to accompany us; accordingly on the twenty-fifth of July we started on the long pull for the Tanana River, nine hundred miles away.

The two steamboats were lashed alongside so our side doors were opposite each other, and our barges were likewise fastened together and pushed ahead of the double boat. For fuel we had several days supply of coal which we hoped would carry us far enough to reach good timber.

As far as the eye could see in all directions was the same dreary expanse of turbid water and low islands and mud flats. Back and forth, now east, now west, now north, then south for three long monotonous days we toiled before we reached the hills of Andrewefski, one hundred and twenty miles from the river's mouth. The islands, which at first were covered with only swamp grass, now were fringed with willows and alders, then balm-of Gilead and cottonwood made their appearances, but it was not until we reached Andrewefski that we saw any birch or spruce, and these were not plentiful until Anvik, two hundred miles further, were reached.

As soon as our supply of coal was exhausted, the fuel question became a most serious one. Nothing but driftwood was available for a long time, and this was most unsatisfactory fuel. It was wet and soggy, hard to cut and worse to split, and almost impossible to burn after it was secured. The Eskimos scattered along the lower river derive their main subsistence from the sale of this wood to steamboats. The standard price is ten dollars per cord or two sacks of flour. Even at this price, wood is hard to get for the steamboats consume large quantities, some of them like the *P.B. Weare* using twenty-four cords daily. The Eskimo rarely, if ever, cuts more than one cord at a time and then waits until his flour or rations are eaten before again going to work!

This mighty Yukon, larger than the Mississippi, muddier than the Missouri, and containing more islands than the St. Lawrence, formerly discharged its waters into the Arctic Ocean, holding nearly a northerly course from Fort Yukon, but since some convulsions of nature threw up the sandstone and conglomerate range which masks its northern bank, its waters surge and fret against the headlands as if impatient at the barrier which turns them in the new direction. If some more prominent crag turns the course of the river into the low alluvial lands on its southern bank, the waters return with increased violence to hurl against the next protruding point. Some of these mighty bends were difficult to pass with our heavy loads. One place just above Anvik must have had a seven mile current and we crawled but slowly up the stream, making scarcely a mile an hour. Another boat, the *May West*, had tried several times before it succeeded, each time being swept back into quieter waters where, after accumulating a new head of steam, it tried again.

We soon found we must systemize our work, so our force was accordingly divided into watches. Six hours per day were spent in cutting and loading wood. This was new work to some of the men, but fortunately we had a few among us who were professionals. Conrad of my party and Frank Gibbs of the *Tanana Chief* were a team by themselves, and the way they dropped the spruces (some of them seventy feet tall) was a wonder to the uninitiated. All the boys were willing to learn, and those who could not acquire the knack of chopping or splitting found work in carrying the prepared wood aboard. Had it not been for the sand flies and mosquitoes, this portion of the work would not have been very arduous. The remainder of the twenty-four hours was divided into two watches of nine hours each. In my party, Brown and Torrance fired the boilers. Conrad and I attended the machinery and stood tricks at the wheel. Bliss looked after the culinary department in great shape. He occasionally secured a mess of currants or cranberries at some stopping place, and surprised us with a concoction with a long, French name, but which made an agreeable change from our steady diet of bacon and beans and fish.

To one who has been accustomed to the Mississippi River with its thriving cities and villages on its banks, rich farms and beautiful wooded slopes, the Yukon would be disappointment. For fifty miles at a stretch we would not see a sign of house or village. Then a scattered Indian fishing camp or two would announce the approach to some mission. At Anvik and Holy Cross were perhaps two score log houses comprising the mission buildings and winter homes of the Eskimo or Indians, but not more than half a dozen missions were located on the river. Occasionally, we passed temporary summer camps of the Indians on some jutting bar or headland where their experience had taught them there was good salmon fishing. Here were erected their drying frames and shed, and these were loaded down with the rich red salmon which the natives had captured from the myriads of fish on their annual migration to the spawning grounds of clear mountain streams.

Between the scattered fishing camps was a wild, unbroken expanse of mountain-covered forests and island with scarcely a trace of human life. The restless river is cutting and undermining the islands, tearing them down in one place only to build anew in another spot lower down, and annually sweeping millions of yards of soil into the Bering Sea, thus rapidly shoaling its basin. The ice gorges in the spring aid in the work of destruction as the scarred and broken tree trunks along the banks could testify. I marked one island where for over a mile every tree had been mowed down slick and clean from the ice movement. Only the split and twisted stumps, fifteen or twenty inches in diameter, were left to mark what once was a heavy growth of spruces. It was this destroying agency of the ice that aided us so much in getting our fuel. The broken and denuded trunks were piled in enormous quantities on the bars and heads of islands, and whenever possible we loaded our boats with the long, slim trunks hauled aboard whole to be cut up as needed.

After passing Nulato, we reached the mouth of the Koyukuk River, one of the Yukon's largest tributaries. Coming in from the north, its length is nearly one thousand miles and over several hundred miles of its length is navigable for steamboats of light draft. Here at the mouth, we found a number of men waiting to secure transportation up the river to Tramway Bar and the gold fields near there.

At this point we also got such discouraging reports about the water at the mouth of the Tanana River that we decided to leave the *Potlatch* and both barges and about half the crew at Koyukuk, the remainder of us taking the *Tanana Chief* and going to Weare for our mail and to investigate for ourselves the state of water at the river's mouth. The distance was two hundred and forty miles. It was a long way to go to the post office you may think! It took us three and one half days to reach Weare where we secured considerable mail but no letters later than May, three months old. From the riverboat *Alice*, just returned from Dawson, we obtained war news as late as July, but did not secure a paper giving any particulars.

At Weare, I met Mr. Prevost, the Episcopal missionary at St. James. We were old acquaintances and I enjoyed several hours visit with him talking over old times and men we both knew. He had made two trips up the Tanana in the winter and thought our project was quite feasible if we could get over the bar at the mouth of the river. He secured a native Indian and on the following day we had no difficulty under his directions of getting up fifteen miles into good water. We turned around at this point and retraced our course, making our run back to Koyukuk in twenty hours.

Now we have reached Weare for the second time, this time with our whole outfit and tomorrow, the twenty-second of August, we start up the Tanana River where we will winter and prospect. As we will be off from the regular mail route, our only way of sending or receiving mail will be by private carrier. Any good opportunity that occurs along this line will be used.

We have but five weeks at most until the river will be un-navigable owing to low water with the coming cold season. Before that time, we hope to be three hundred miles up the Tanana and to have secured a safe anchorage for our boats. Log camps must be built against the approach of the cold weather, and a plentiful supply of fresh meat and fish stored for our winter's use. So during our next month or two we will be busy and have little time for letter writing."

At this point I quote from a letter written by Ed Conrad and in it he describes in a pithy manner our three months trip up the river from Weare.

Fort Chena, Alaska
October 1, 1898

....Today I avail myself of what will be the last opportunity until next spring to send a letter back to civilization and home. First of all, let me assure all dear relatives and friends that we are well and happy. We are now about three hundred and twenty-five miles above Weare and here we intend to make our winter's headquarters.

In about two more days we will have completed our cabin which is fifteen by twenty-three feet inside. Fred Currier and I whipsawed the lumber for it and also for floor and bunks. Only those who have undertaken such a job can form anything like an accurate idea of the immense amount of labor required. Our cabin is alongside that of the boys of the *Tanana Chief* who accompanied us to this place. The two cabins are connected by a covered wood shed so that in passing from one cabin to another we won't have to step out of doors.

Words cannot express the full sense of our appreciation of the many kindnesses extended to us by the boys of the *Chief*. In my last letter I told you how we happened to come together and we have not been separated since. They have great confidence in our leader, Currier, and are determined to stick by us, but so far we are the gainers by our close relationship. They helped us out of the greatest mishap that has thus far befallen us, in a way that makes us forever indebted to them. To arrive at our present location, we had to come up the Tanana River two hundred and fifteen miles, and then up the Chena River another hundred or so, or as far as a steamer could go on account of the low water. We had not gotten more than well started on this trip when a part of our boat machinery, the injector, gave out and prevented us from getting water into the boiler. Dirty water was no doubt the cause of the trouble. The boys of the *Chief* took us in tow for about one hundred miles, where we laid by the *Potlatch* in a small creek or mouth of a back slough, and all hands doubled up on the *Tanana Chief.*

From that time on we had a hard, long struggle to get the Chief up the rapids and over the many swift currents. We had to "line" and resort to other schemes to baffle the relentless force of the heavy and ever onrushing waters, and I thank the Lord we are all alive and well.

I know it will disappoint some of my friends should I not attempt a longer description of this country, but as we have only seen those small portions of it that lie on either side of the rivers we have travelled, I can give no very accurate information, nor will I be able to do so until after we start our prospecting tours which will probably be in the spring.

As to weather, I can say that up to the present we have had little to complain of. Two light snow falls within the past fortnight were just enough to cover the ground and it freezes a little every night. The days are about as long here now as they are at home, but are shortening fast. The moon shines brightly every night, while the splendor of the Northern Lights is beyond comparison with anything I ever witnessed in Wisconsin.

The Indians have found us, and nearly every day some of them come to trade with us. Their wares consist principally of moose meat, dried fish and foot wear. The moose meat looks and tastes like beef. We hope to procure our own game in a few days as there is lots of it in this neighborhood. Moose and bear trails here are like cow trails in a meadow, while pheasants are also plentiful. When we finish our cabins, we will unpack our guns and go on a foraging expedition. Fred Currier and I and some of the *Tanana Chief* boys will go up the mountains and taking our guns with us will combine business with pleasure. We will build little stopping places or cabins about ten miles apart on the way up. It makes no difference when Fred goes, I must go with him!

Speaking of shooting reminds me that some of the boys who have attempted to use their rifles have had trouble with them. Tony, the cook of the Tanana Chief, went out one day and about twenty rods from the cabin saw a bear standing erect. He first thought it was a man and did not shoot. When the bear got down and commenced to run through the grass, Tony shot quickly but missed his game. A second shot hung fire and at the third attempt the lever got stuck and prevented the gun's further use! Two of the other men have had similar experience with their guns. Fred tells me he had no trouble with arms in his former trip and pins his faith on the old Winchester as the most reliable gun for this cold climate.

I must tell you of a party by whom we are sending out these letters. The Indians brought one of them, Lieut. Castner, to our cabin not long ago and he told us a tale of thrilling misfortune and adventure. They were a party of government surveyors and were descending a river on a raft when a swift current swept them under a low hanging tree, sweeping the raft clean, even their boots were lost, the men having taken them off while standing on the raft. They escaped with nothing except what they had on their backs. They had to subsist on berries and dead salmon that lined the bank of the stream. Making their way finally to an Indian camp, they were rescued from starvation and Lieut. Castner engaged the Indians to take him up the Chena to where the Indians told him 'there were white men with boats,' with the hope of help out of the country before winter set in. We helped them out with as much as we could spare, a boat, shoes, socks, and provisions to last them until they could reach the government garrison at Weare. Hope they make it out, though Fred warned them that they would have to run night and day if they expected to get across the Yukon before it freezes up. Lieut. Castner's feet were quite badly frozen when he got to us. If this letter reaches you, you will know that the Lieutenant got out as we are sending our mail by him."

The *Tanana Chief* and both our scows were anchored in a back water channel of the Chena, the upper opening of which was blocked by an immense logjam. This insured perfect safety to the boats from the spring floods. The *Potlatch* had been left some miles below in a similar anchorage. We were still many miles below the headwaters of the Chena and its tributaries. It was to reach these mountain streams that we now turned.

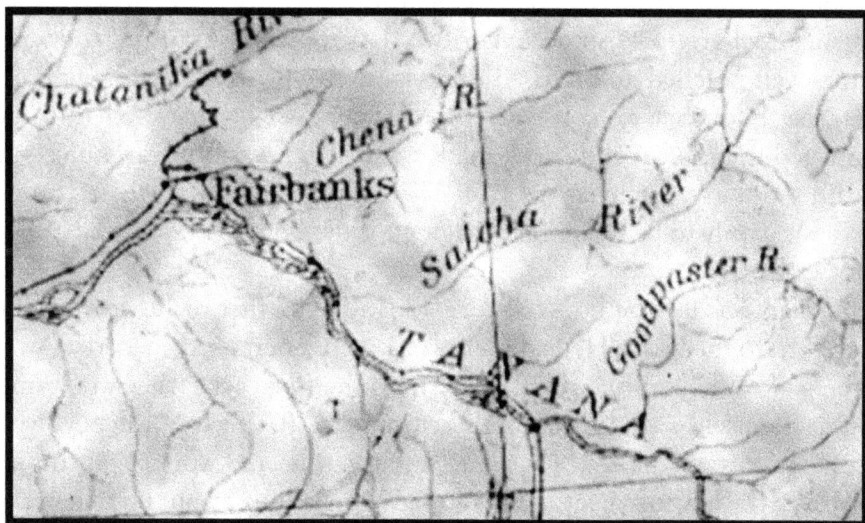

Interior Rivers

Chapter 24
We Establish Fort Independence

All the way up the Chena I had been panning the heads of bars and everywhere were indications of gold. Usually light, flaky particles, as would be expected as the heavier gold if there were any would be left far above, appeared in the pans. Once I got a dollar of quite coarse gold. We surely felt we were going in the right direction as by the middle of October the pans continued favorable.

By mid-October the rivers were frozen over and there was sufficient snow for sledding. Ed Conrad and I, with Frank Gibbs and Tony Olsen, set out up river. We took two sleds loaded with bedding, camp stove, and outfit and provisions for two months. Following the ice on the main river wherever the course of the latter was fairly direct, we would cut across the timbered neck to avoid some large oxbend. These "cutoffs" we marked plainly with blazed trees or other signs for the boys that were slowly following in our rear.

About ten miles from the boat, we made our first stop and pitched our tent in a sheltered group of spruces. For two days we worked cutting and rolling up logs well notched and mossed. It was a twelve by sixteen cabin with walls seven feet high that we constructed. A flat roof of logs covered with moss completed the roof. A rude door made of split logs was hung on hinges—this was Ed Conrad's particular job. There were no windows as these stopping places were only to be temporary lodging for the boys as they moved our outfit forward.

Our plan was for the boys to move a load to the first cache, leave it there and return to the boats. Hence, twenty miles a day, ten of them loaded, would be the goal. When all the goods were up to the first cache, they would move up to it themselves, and repeat the performance. In this way, the boys would have a comfortable place to sleep and save the time and work of putting up a tent as we, the advance guard, were doing. We planned to put up one of these stopping camps about every ten miles. The first load from the boat arrived just as we finished camp number one.

Arrival of Potlatch Party, and two of the Tanana Chief Party, at Camp they called #10, where they built Fort Independence. Frederick Currier at extreme top center. The men are wearing Mosquito netting from their hats. Their dog Bella is carrying a a pack. 1899. (Amy June Currier Jorgensen Collection)

We could hear Tom and Ollie coming across the neck and heard Tom calling, "Mush you malemute or I warm your hide!"

Then came Ollie with another rangy Indian dog, and Bliss brought up the rear with "Stop-the-Clock" or it sounded something like that. The boys had secured the dogs from the Indians, or rather I had purchased them for them before we left the boat. In the old Circle City days, the standard price of one Indian dog was one 50# sack of flour. When the Indians came to the boat and I had selected the dogs wanted, I had laid out a sack of flour for each dog as usual.

Their spokesman, Jasper, who could talk a little English, looked at the flour then at the dogs and said, "Dawson, dogs $100. Flour, how much?"

"One hundred dollars," I gravely replied.

"Oh, all right," said Jasper and the trade was consummated.

The boys estimated it would take ten trips each before they would get up all the outfit from the boats. In that case, we would be far ahead of them, and in fact we did not see any of them again until Christmas. Day after day we toiled forward, stopping two days at each camp to put up a log shelter, then on to the next. In all, we erected ten camps, then coming to favorable looking gulches we erected more permanent dwellings and for the first time since leaving the boats slept under wooden walls.

The weather had been growing colder, much colder. Several times the mercury in our thermometer was frozen and snow was now about two feet deep. It was impossible to pull a loaded sled through this amount of unbroken snow, so I adopted the plan usually followed by the old-timers. With snowshoes, Ed and I, or Frank and I, struck out ahead, going the ten miles and locating the next stopping place. We would take turns breaking trail, the rear walker "staggering" any inequalities left by the leader. Thus we had a smooth trail or trough about eighteen inches wide and crushed down a foot or more. On returning, we retraced our steps in the same trail, now frozen hard. By morning, this trail would bear up under a heavy load.

I mentioned that we had lived in tents during all this period. It is surprising how comfortable a tent can be made if one knows how. First, the snow was tramped flat with our snowshoes. That avoided any rough spots on the ground. Next, the tent was set up and pegged down in the snow. As there are no winds in the interior in the winter, pegs in the snow were sufficient to hold the canvas. A log was rolled on the tent flap and then banked with snow. So much for the outside. A layer of flat spruce limbs a foot thick was spread over the snow inside the tent and over these boughs a moose skin with the long, four inch hair side uppermost was placed. Yes, we had shot a moose and the hide nearly covered the entire floor of the tent. The beds filled one end of the tent. Here we placed more boughs, our wolf skin robes, and blankets to form our sleeping quarters.

Our Yukon stove with its collapsible stovepipe was set on two green logs and when the birch wood fire was crackling and the tent door flap tied, we were as warm and cozy as one could desire. We ate our meals sitting on the foot of our beds and holding our plates in our laps.

Caribou were frequently crossing the trails going from one side of the long valley to the ridges on the other side in search of caribou moss or lichens which was their favorite winter food. We shot several for meat.

I had obtained quite favorable bar prospects below a six mile long gulch coming from a high domed peak that reminded me of Mastodon in the Circle City region. We decided that this was a good location for a permanent camp. Frank named it Independence Gulch, and the houses we erected we called Fort Independence. We built two cabins, one for the *Tanana Chief* boys and one for ourselves. We then began sinking shafts, thawing them down with fires as I had done on former occasions. In fact, we started work on several nearby gulches. If nothing were found here, we could reach other outlying gulches in the spring.

About Christmas time, the advance team of our freighters came into camp and soon the whole outfit was safely stored. The boys were tanned and hardened by the cold and exposure, but not one of them had had a sick day or any accident. On Christmas day we had a plum pudding that Bliss had secured in Seattle nine months before! It was a touch of home. I remember we all got quite sentimental talking about home ties and friends, wondering if Lieut. Castner got out with our letters and if the folks had heard from us yet. Sid Warner celebrated his 21st birthday by smoking a pipe for the first time. His father had promised him a thousand dollars if he would not smoke until he reached his 21st birthday, and Sid faithfully followed the request, but he had laid in a generous stock of Piper Harsick and opened a package early on Christmas morning.

Chapter 25
A Busy Year
1899

The boys certainly enjoyed a rest from the trail, but sinking shafts, hoisting thawed dirt, and cutting wood for the fires were no sinecure either, especially those short, cold winter days. I had a spirit thermometer that was graduated to 72 degrees below zero and once or twice in January the tube was nearly, or quite, empty, the spirit having shrunk into the bulb.

So far none of the shaft holes had shown any pay that warranted further work. We got out some gold, of course, but not the bonanza we were hoping for. As the days grew longer and the cold less intense, we made several trips to the summit of the ranges on either side, planning our summer prospecting trips.

Some caribou had been seen crossing the gulches at frequent times during the winter. These were small bands but gave us plenty of fresh meat, but with the warmer days toward spring the caribou herds increased in large numbers. The northward migration had begun. One Sunday morning we were sitting outside the cabin enjoying the sun when Tom suddenly exclaimed, "See there!"

Following the direction indicated by his finger, we saw a lone caribou dashing down the opposite slope of the gulch and coming almost directly toward our cabin. This slope had been burned over a few years previously and the surface was bare except for a few dry stubs of trees, so we had an unobstructed view. It was unusual to see a lone animal this way, as the caribou travel in bands for mutual protection. Nearer and nearer came the fleeing animal.

"Look, there it is!" shouted Bliss, "a great wolf after the caribou!"

Sure enough, a great, gaunt wolf nearly as white as snow was only a few rods behind the frightened animal and rapidly gaining upon its quarry. Ollie seized his rifle and we all waited breathless for the outcome. Where the caribou would have to cross the gulch, the bank at the far side was fully ten feet high. With a flying leap, the animal cleared the bank and landed fully halfway across the frozen surface of the stream. But the wolf was equally quick. Its leap brought it close on the rear of the caribou and before the latter could recover from the effect of its leap, the wolf seized the crazed animal by the flank, jerked it backward and the next second had cut the caribou's throat and the deed was done. No, not done, for Ollie's rifle rang out and the wolf rolled over dead. It was an old she-wolf, thin and nearly white from age, and carrying nine pups nearly ready to be dropped. It seemed almost incredible that a creature so old and in that condition as she was could have lone-handed captured a fleeing caribou.

Spring finally arrived with its ever recurring miracle of rushing, pulsing life from death. The waters were running, trees pushing out leaves, flowers blooming and the air was full of returning birds from the southland on their migration northward.

A sad incident had taken place just before the spring breakup. Joe Morgan had died and we had laid him away on a point overlooking the beautiful stream. Joe was a Civil War veteran, and while older than the rest of us, had endeared himself to all by his cheery disposition and unfailing willingness to lend his help in any emergency. He was stricken with dropsy early in the winter and gradually grew worse. He was a member of the *Tanana Chief* party and their Dr. Fuller did everything possible under the circumstances, but we had to say good-by to Joe. A glass goblet that Joe had carried through the Civil

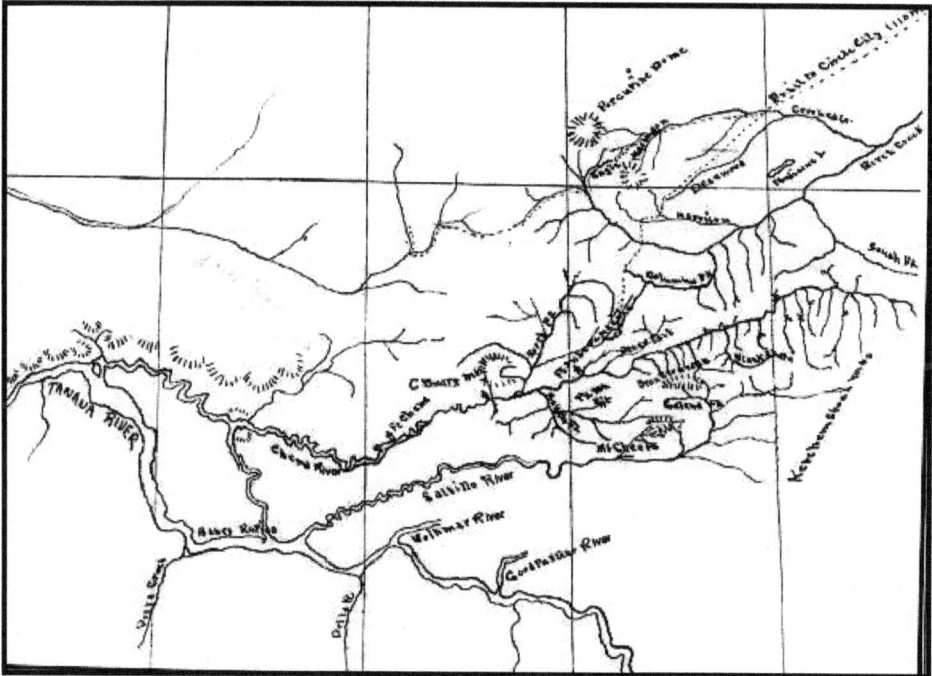

A hand drawn map by Frederick Currier.

War was with him, and Ed took charge of it and would carry the glass out and see that it was returned to Joe's widow.

The summer was spent in prospecting on gulches of the Chena. Our plan consisted of dividing into small parties and, with a week or two of provisions, we went out in different directions, returning to headquarters for provisions when the supply taken was exhausted. The Black Shale, a tributary coming into the Chena, had been fairly promising with five cent pans being frequently obtained plus some fairly coarse gold. We decided to pin our faith on that creek and give it a thorough prospecting in the winter by burning shafts to crosscut the gulch in two or three places.

In July, 1899 Frank Gibbs and Tony Olsen made a trip to Circle City for mail and also to take out our letters. We had left directions before leaving St. Michael for our mail to be forwarded to Circle City. The boys were gone two weeks and came back with a wealth of letters and papers. Among them were copies of "The Outlook" which I had subscribed for before leaving Wisconsin. It gave us a complete history of the Spanish American War and the capture of Manila by Commodore Dewey. A letter from home also told me my brother Harry had lost his life there. A letter from him, over a year old, told of his joining the Minnesota regiment and sailing for the Philippines.

As the summer of 1899 drew to a close, the boys began to get restless in our failure to find really good paying gulches. The *Tanana Chief* men decided to go down to their boat and cruise up to Dawson. Oliver Torrance, Charles Bliss and Tom Brown also felt the Dawson call. Ed Conrad and I and Frank Gibbs and Tony Olsen voted for another year along the creeks to the south of us that headed against the Forty Mile River that we had not yet visited.

We all turned in and whipsawed lumber and built a couple of scows suitable for floating down the river as far as the steamboats. Our outfits were equitably divided and we saw the boys off, wished them bon voyage and turned back to our work. Rather lonesome it seemed at first, but Frank and Tony moved into our cabin and so we were full house once more.

We were fairly close to one of the salmon spawning grounds on a nearby tributary to the south, and we never tired of watching the fish. According to authorities who were versed in the history of the life of the Chinook or king salmon, the noblest of all the finny tribe, these return to the same waters where they were hatched four years before. There was usually a deep pool both below and above the spawning bed. A pair of salmon, for they had already selected mates, would approach the riffle, the female in the lead. She would scoop out a long, shallow trench, flipping the sand and pebbles to one

Stan Gibson and Judd Elliot yarding wood.

side, then with a few resounding thumps of her body would eject a stream of eggs. The male, following close behind, would fertilize the eggs then both fish would pass on to the upper pool to recuperate only to return time after time until the eggs were all deposited. Then both fish, their life cycle complete, would swim up to the bank or into shallow water to die. These spawning beds were harvest ground for bears, and bruin waxed fat on the big king salmon. Walking into the water, a flip of the paws sent the fish flying to the bank where the cubs that accompanied their mother pounced on the fish, quarreling and scuffling although the supply was inexhaustible.

Seeing the bears so busy, I bethought myself that it would be well for us to lay in a supply of fish for winter, both for our dogs and ourselves. We had a small boat that we had brought up from the *Potlatch* and in this, with one man to paddle and the other wielding a spear, we spent a week fishing and took in over two tons. It was necessary to pick only the healthy fish that had not yet spawned. It was exciting work as many of the fish weighed 35 to 40 pounds. The boys would split the fish down the back cutting out the heavy backbone. The two sides were then hung up on a string of poles and a slow fire, made both to smoke the meat and to aid in the drying, was started below them.

Swarms of grayling followed the salmon, feasting on the eggs that were not

Wolverine Gulch, Chena River, where *"a good prospect was found"*
Their cabin is in the center of the photograph.
George Brandon Photograph Album, 1898-1900
(See also: November 26, 1899 and February 25, 1900.)

quickly covered by sand or gravel. We took the grayling with bait and flies. They made a very nice pan fried fish, especially the half pound size. The flesh is firm and hard, white in color. The backbone and ribs come out together similar to that of the brook trout. The grayling has scales that have to be scraped off, and there is a very prominent back fin. In all our prospecting trips, the grayling played quite a prominent part; it generally required but a few minutes casting a fly to secure a mess.

On one of our prospecting trips we had taken the boat and gone up the Chena about ten miles, leaving it for our return from a week's exploration. Coming home and floating quietly down the stream we jumped three moose, two cows and a big bull. The cows dashed off to one side, but the bull came splashing directly upstream toward us. The wind was upstream so he could not scent us. On he came. One of the boys had a rifle and fired but made a clean miss. On came the moose, startled and harried by the noise, but still not seeing us! So close he came that I was about to step out of the boat thinking his next plunge would be in our midst, but just then the big animal caught a whiff or glimpse of us and sprang to one side. When a rifle shot had laid him low, we estimated his weight at 1,500 pounds. It was the largest moose I had ever seen! As it was getting late in the fall, we could save the meat and freeze it, so we built a raft and floated the dressed carcass down to our camp.

I might relate another moose incident here at this point. Ed and I had been out for a month, prospecting. In fact, we stayed away so long that all our provisions were exhausted. A long tramp brought us home about three o'clock, and hungry too. Tony and Frank were away somewhere too, and the camp was empty.

I said to Ed, "You just crack up some wood and get a fire ready and I will go back up on the divide and get a caribou so we can have some fresh meat."

Ed was agreeable and I started up the trail to the divide, about a mile away. I jumped a bunch of caribou almost first thing on gaining the top, and shot an unusually large buck. I cut out the saddle and getting it up on my back I made off down the trail thinking of a good supper Ed and I would have. Upon coming in sight of the cabin there was no smoke coming out of the chimney, and rounding the end to the door, there was no Ed, no fire, no sign of supper having been started. Dropping the meat, I set my rifle against the cabin wall, picked up the ax to break some wood for a fire, when smash! Crash! A big bull moose came dashing around the end of the cabin. He had apparently been trailing me down the mountain pass. Luckily he hadn't come on me a moment sooner. As he crashed by, I seized my rifle and downed him by a lucky shot. He fell not fifty yards from the door! Just then Ed came hurrying down the gulch.

"Come on, Fred!" he called. "I have just killed six caribou. I heard them, when I was getting wood and stalked them down!"

"Go get them yourself," I responded laughingly. "I make my game walk in!" and I pointed to the dead moose.

Ed could hardly believe the story I told him about it. Well, of course, we had a job saving all the meat of the moose and those caribou, but cold weather set in and the meat was safe.

Chapter 26
Visitors from the Jennie M.

Soon after my moose experience we had unexpected callers. A party of men came up the gulch and I at once recognized them as some we had met in St. Michael two years before. Their boat was the *Jennie M.* It seems they had gone up the Koyukuk River the first year, but not finding any pay gold had returned and gone up the Yukon as far as Circle City where they had learned of my whereabouts. Frank and Tony had been over for the mail about that time, so the word had gone around where I was located. The *Jennie M.* had followed up the Tanana and Chena Rivers and was now tied about six miles below us. There were ten or twelve men in their party, but they were "not much on the prospect" as the sourdoughs say. However, we were glad to see them and had many visits back and forth.

By late October it was time to lay in a winter stock of meat, and the caribou run was on. The *Jennie M.* people came up to see us and when we told them of our decision to winter in again, they too set out to stock up, for of necessity they would have to winter on the Chena. The water was already too low for their steamboat to make the run out. I gave them pointers on building a safe cache, warning them to be sure the logs were green, otherwise a wolverine would cut into the cache through dry wood.

We decided to make two caches for ourselves, one near the home place, the other about twenty miles up stream at the Black Shale. I also told our boys we would put some extra meat up as I was a little doubtful about the *Jennie M.* making a successful job of their hunt. It was not a question of killing the game, for one of their hunters was Sam Entrigen. A fine shot, Sam had been with Admiral Peary on two expeditions, on one of them crossing Greenland, being Peary's only companion on that memorable trip. It nearly broke Entrigen's heart that he was not allowed to make the final and successful expedition to the pole, but Sam had had an accident and Peary did not think it advisable to let him make the attempt.

We put up thirty caribou, two moose and a couple of nice fat bears. One of these last had been feasting on blueberries and the lard had a faint blueberry flavor. We especially liked this for frying doughnuts and the boys were always calling on Tony to make some of those blueberry fritters, as they called them.

We very nearly had a serious accident on one of those days. We had dropped a couple of caribou on a bar across the river. Ice had formed but not completely closing the channel as yet. Not wishing to wade up to our necks in the icy water, we found a place where we thought by cutting a leaning tree the top would bridge the gap to the other side. Ed felled the tree, a spruce, but the bushy top still lacked a few feet of reaching the opposite bank.

"Cut a small one, Ed," I directed, "and we can push it on past the top to the bank."

This was done, and taking the top in my arms I edged my way out on the first tree over the rushing water which at this point was six or seven feet deep. All would have gone well but Frank, who was carrying the other end of the tree I was holding, stumbled and in falling managed to give the tree such a twist that I was pushed backwards into the water. Immediately below us was a deep pool and its surface was frozen over for a considerable space. Were I carried under the ice this narrative would never have been written! I went under water, but coming up, gasping, a wet branch of the first fallen tree swished across my face. Of course, I grasped it instinctively and held on until both Ed and Frank worked their way out on the top and caught me by the arms and hauled me to safety. My clothes began to freeze instantly, but the boys knew what to do in such an emergency. Tony had already stripped some birch bark from a nearby tree and had started a fire. He made a roaring one too. I was stripped to my underclothes and stockings and kept as close to the fire as safety allowed, being turned round and round like a roasting apple. The boys wrung out the wet clothing and hung these before the fire too. An hour later I was clothed again and never suffered a particle from the wetting. We completed the bridge and secured the caribou without any further mishap.

When the *Jennie M.* boys went to visit their cache shortly before Christmas time, they had found that not a shred of meat remained. Instead of building the log house on high green posts as I had advised, they had followed directions in a book someone owned. A tall tree had been selected, stripped of its branches for twenty feet, then a ring of slanting poles braced against the tree. Each pole held the dressed and frozen carcass of a caribou. Twenty in all had been put up. The skins had covered the whole in tent fashion. The book had assured them that neither bird nor beast would molest meat so cached. I had shaken my head when they had told me of their plan, but they went ahead with it anyway. When they went for meat, they discovered the cured hides had been torn to strips by the ravens and the wolverines and wolves had cut down and devoured the meat, even the bones were eaten. We gave them some of our plentiful supply and so helped them out over the rest of the winter.

We were all invited to the *Jennie M.* for Christmas dinner 1899, and their cook, for they had a professional, had a stuffed and baked "fool hen" for each man. One of the men mentioned that it was a wonderful land, that all the way up the rivers they had found splendid green peas growing on the mud flats and they had feasted on them. The history of those peas was interesting. When we bought our outfit I had ordered a sack of dried split peas, planning them for soup. By mistake the order had been filled with garden peas. They had accidentally fallen overboard one day in the upper river and as we did not especially care for them, we let them go. The bag had burst and the peas had washed up on the mud flats and had been furnishing the luxury of fresh peas to the *Jennie M.* men!

Chapter 27

Census Year
1900

Chatanika Cronies.

Shortly after the first of the year, two more men showed up. They were Pete Nelson and Jake Metz. They had come in a row boat from Dawson to Weare in the past fall. There Mr. Prevost had told them of the three steamboats that had ascended the Tanana. Pete had felt it was worth getting an outfit at Weare and wintering with us, and so they did. It took so little in those days to turn a man to a new site for possible gold; a hint, a rumor and he was off, a hundred or maybe a thousand miles. Pete and Jake arrived as we were packing up for a trip southward, onto the next large tributary, the Saltito or Saltchocket as the Indians called it. Jake and Pete were eager to go with us, so all six of us with heavy packs, and our several dogs also loaded down, crossed the swamp, icy flat on the far side of the Chena and started the long pull up the nose toward the divide beyond. Frequent rests were made and we had lunch before reaching the top. While eating and resting we spied a moose feeding in a little grassy meadow in the gulch just below. Jake was all eager to go down and kill it. He had never shot any big game.

"No, Jake," I cautioned, "I never kill any game that I do not need or can't take care of. If you should kill that moose we would just have to let it lie there. Wait until we get over the divide, then you may kill a caribou for we will want some fresh meat."

"All right," agreed Jake, "I see the point."

Crossing the divide and a short way down the far side, we sat down to consider where best to strike the stream below us. All at once Jake exclaimed, "See there, there's a caribou!" He pointed to a clump of willows just on the fringe of the timber and about half a mile below us.

"I don't see any caribou, Jake," I said after carefully scrutinizing the scene.

"Yes, yes, right this side of that clump of willows is a caribou!" Jake insisted.

"All right, Jake, if you see a caribou, go get him!" I replied.

"I'll go too," said Frank.

The boys dropped their packs and hurried off down the grade. I had a pair of field glasses and I had discovered that Jake's caribou was a brown bear feasting on winter ripe blueberries! Passing the glass to the other boys I said, "I think we will see some fun when Jake reaches his caribou."

However, I took the packs off the dogs for they were good bear dogs and I imagined they might be needed. We held them in leash, however. While the boys had gone down the slope, the bear had worked around on the far side of the clump of willows. Discovering this, the two men separated, Frank going to the left, and Jake to the right. Jake was the one who found the game first, and coming plump on the bear he must have been a surprised Dutchman! In his fright and haste, and like most amateurs in shooting downhill, he over shot, just nicking one of the bear's ears. It was a brown, bald-faced bear and they are fighters. The Indians will seldom tackle them.

With a rush and a roar the bear charged Jake, who, firing a second shot that also missed, dropped his gun and ran for his life, the bear in close pursuit. The moment I heard the first shot I turned the dogs loose and they went flying down toward the scene below. We hurriedly followed. Frank, hearing the shots and the commotion, rushed back and just in time put a telling shot into the bear's neck as with a sweep of his paw he nearly stripped the pants from off poor Jake and sent him flying. The dogs too reached the arena and aided in finishing the fight. Jake was a laughable sight, but fortunately unhurt except for his pride. The next day he had the misfortune to be chased by a mother bear with cubs, and as he expressed it, "I no more bears want to see!"

We spent a fortnight on the Saltchocket, but without results as far as gold was concerned. Prospects on bars and exposed bedrock did not show up as well as what we had found on the Chena. We returned to our headquarters and spent much of the rest of the winter and spring working the Black Shale.

Our winter work was well under way when one day a dog team and a solitary driver appeared on the scene. Who should it prove to be but my old Circle City acquaintance, Windy Jim.

"Hello, Fred," he cried, "I've had a heck of a time finding you! Been two weeks since I left Circle. Thought I never would get over some of these ranges!"

"But why should you try to find me, Jim?" I asked. "I am not lost!"

"Of course not," replied Jim, "but this is census year and I am census enumerator for this part of the world."

To be sure, it was the year 1900 and Uncle Sam was counting the noses of his subjects even in this faraway frozen land. We made Windy welcome and he spent several days with us before leaving on his 300 mile lonesome trip to Valdez and the coast. After leaving us and the *Jennie M.* boys, he would not see another white man until he reached Valdez; 450 miles he would travel to enumerate sixteen men!

Weeks later, on his return trip to Circle City, this same Windy Jim brought us all the news of the various camps and he regaled us with word about all of them, but the BIG ITEM of the year was the discovery of beach gold at Nome! While we had been up in the Tanana, the rich diggings on Anvil Creek had been located, Nome had sprung up and while building a trading post on the edge of the tundra the beach diggings had been struck. Old Cummings had panned out $3,000 in one day and the beach was rich for twenty miles! All Dawson and Circle were going in the spring.

"The country up there is just lousy with gold," so Jim rattled on, and we had caught some of his enthusiasm as well.

"Might as well go too," commented Tony.

We figured the *Jennie M.* boys would go and decided to ask if we could go along with them. That was agreeable with them, and we planned to go in the spring as soon as the water ran deep enough for the boat to get out. But there were several months before spring would arrive, and we returned to our work on the Black Shale.

Chapter 28
Off to Nome!
1900

As the longer days of spring approached, we moved our outfits down to the old headquarters where we had left the *Tanana Chief* and scows. Of course, the *Chief* was gone, but our cabins were still intact. Here we would wait until the *Jennie M.* came along, which we figured would be at least a month later. As we had not brought much meat with us, we went hunting in the woods which contained much taller spruces than in the upper regions where we had been. The trees were full of fool hens and ruffled grouse, and the willow ptarmigans were found along the bars. We killed many of the fowl, using the choice portions for ourselves and feeding the dogs the remainder. Tony kept a record of the birds and declared the score was one thousand in the thirty day period! We were certainly tired of fool hens by the time the whistle of the *Jennie M.* sounded.

We piled aboard and waved a final farewell to our homes of the past years. Fifty miles below was the Potlatch and we planned to take it in tow down to the Yukon where we hoped to repair the defective injectors, or secure new ones from some steamboat, so as to use our own craft for the trip down to St. Michael and Nome. As we approached the point where we had left the *Potlatch* we espied it swinging at her harness.

"But what the dickens is that!" ejaculated Ed, pointing to a great barrier of sticks, brush and stones barring the outlet where the boat was moored.

"That, my boy, is a beaver dam," I replied. "The cunning rascals have penned in the *Potlatch.*"

Well, of all things," said Tony, "what did they do that for?"

"Oh, I imagine it is just one of their ordinary dams," I replied, "and our boat just happened to be swimming on the water they dammed up for their own purposes."

"How are we going to get the *Potlatch* out of there?" demanded Frank. "Looks to me like quite a job."

"We'll have to tear the dam to pieces, if we can," I explained.

The *Jennie M.* tied up just below the beaver dam and their men willingly lent us their assistance. Donning rubber boots, we all sallied out to do the job. The top of the dam was about four or five feet wide, but the width of the structure rapidly increased below the water. The dam was a mixed tangle of sticks, small logs, brush, stones, gravel and mud, all packed and bound together in inextricable confusion. We pulled and tugged and pried, throwing the loosened pieces to one side. Breaking up the top that was above water was not so difficult, but our troubles really began when we had to fish out the debris below water. By nightfall we had a channel with only about a foot of water in it. We would need three and a half feet to float the *Potlatch.*

"Another day will do it," said Tony, but I was not so sanguine.

I was rudely awakened early in the morning by Tony shouting in my ear, "Fred, Fred, get up quick and come out here! Those beavers have built up their dam again while we were sleeping!"

It was true. The cunning, industrious animals had almost undone our day's work!

"All that hard labor gone for nothing," groaned Gibbs.

"We must build a fire and set a watch," I said, "or they will repeat the performance."

Another hard day's work expired, and that night we built a bonfire and took turns keeping it going while watching for the beavers. We built the fire on one side of the dam, using the dry portions above water for fuel. Ed took the first watch. I relieved him at twelve o'clock.

"See anything, Ed?" I asked as I came up to take his place.

"I heard some splashing out in the pond next to the boat," he replied, "and saw one or two heads bobbing in the water."

"At three o'clock I called Tony and turned in for a few hours' more sleep. The boys were eating breakfast when I joined them.

"All o.k. this morning," said Tony. "Guess we have the best of the rascals."

But Tony exulted too soon. Another long, wet, hard day's work and we had but a two foot channel. At that depth it was impossible to chop or saw a log under water and even had it been off the rocks, gravel and sand rendered such efforts abortive. It was nothing but pull, pry and tug to loosen a chunk, duck into the water to get a rock and heave it out.

"Blast the brutes," exclaimed Frank, who, in pulling out a stick that stuck, had the unfortunate experience of having it suddenly release and tip him backwards into the cold water!

"I do believe that nothing but dynamite will clear this obstruction," said Entrigen. "We have hardly accomplished anything all day and we are all wet and tired."

It was a fact. Knowing that the *Jennie M.* men were anxious to be on their way, although they expressed a willingness to stay with us and see us through the job, I reluctantly gave orders to abandon the work. Some other way and some other time must see the rescue of the *Potlatch* if ever it were to be done. The beavers won! At this point I will say that several years later upon the discovery of the Fairbanks mines, I sent men with dynamite up to the *Potlatch*. They were amazed to see the beavers' barrier. They blew up the dam, floated the boat to Fairbanks and the boiler and machinery in the boat were used in the mines at Fairbanks.

A few hours run the next morning brought us to the mouth of the Chena River. On a level flat a few miles above the mouth was to be located the town of Fairbanks, soon one of the richest mining camps in Alaska. We had stopped at this point on going up the river. It had been a question of whether to proceed up the Chena or try one of the rivers farther up the Tanana. At this point, the Tanana makes a great bend, and lying in the curve of the bend was one of those domes that are so characteristic of the interior mountain ranges of Alaska. The dome was back some ten or twelve miles from the river and there were no streams of any size coming down from it on the Tanana side. Had we only known, on the far side of this dome were creeks leading into the Tolovana River and also into the south fork of the Chena that were rich in placer gold.

The finding of these places was a romantic episode. A man named Felix Pedro had gone prospecting one summer from Circle City. Crossing the divide at the head of Hoggum, he wandered on, fording creeks and following divides until one day he found a stream with coarse gold and nuggets. He took back a goodly sample to show the truth of his report. Of course, other prospectors followed, Pedro leading the way. Unfortunately, he was one of those men who have no good sense of locality, and he soon was completely lost. All summer he and the men following him searched in vain for the fabulous stream he had told about. Sometime later, another prospector did run onto the creek and found Pedro's stakes and workings. The creek at least was given the original discover's name so that he had something to show for his long search. But we were all ignorant of these matters that were to come to pass in this area a couple of years later.

As we sailed out of the Chena into the Tanana, Ed called back to the river we were leaving, "Good-by Chena. You have given us a merry chase, but some-day, old lady, you will give up your secret that you have kept hidden form us."

Two days later we tied up at Weare, on the opposite bank of the Yukon. There had been nothing but a mission at this point when we went up the Tanana two years previously, but now there was a government military post, with barracks, and a dozen buildings. A company of soldiers were drilling, and later in the day we heard a band play "Home, Sweet Home." I do not know if the music had anything to do with it, but Ed announced that he must go home that fall. He would run up to Dawson on the *Jennie M.*, as that group had decided to do, spend the summer there, but would have to go out in the fall. I did not try to dissuade him, but I knew I would miss him terribly.

Frank and Tony also caught the Dawson fever, so the whole party put off leaving me alone on the banks at Weare, and they asked, even begged me to go along too, but I had started for Nome and to Nome I must go. I certainly had a lonesome feeling as I saw the boat and all of my companions of the last few years disappear from sight, but not for long. Just then someone tapped me on the shoulder and said, "Hello Fred, how goes it?"

I wheeled, then grasped the extended hand. It was Walter Watson, one of my old Circle City friends. I had not seen him for four years.

"Come over to my tent," invited Walter, "and we'll eat and talk too."

And did we talk! I related all our experiences, telling of the *Potlatch*, our two years on the Chena and now here waiting a chance to get to Nome. Walter had worked in the mines at Dawson, and the last year had made a little money mining on a Baker Creek, a tributary of the Tanana, a short distance up from the mouth of that river. Walter had a boat, a fairly good river boat, large enough to carry two persons and their camp equipment. He proposed what we run down the river in it to St. Michael and from that point get across to Nome by an ocean steamer. I fell in with his plan at once and we left in the morning for the one thousand mile run.

We made long days of it, in fact drifted all night at times. We occasionally camped on a bar and got a good rest and sleep. When we approached the delta area we had to be very watchful not to get drawn into some of the side channels that would wander off through the tundra and willows. These channels divided into smaller and smaller streams until at last all were lost in some lake or swampy region that was impassible either by boat or by foot. We later heard of two men that did get into such a predicament and were ten days working back to the main channel of the Yukon. No such fate befell us, and we passed out through the Aphoon mouth and saw Point Ramanzof thirty-two miles distant showing across Pastolik Bay.

"Now," said Walter, "what say? Shall we head straight across, or follow the shore line?"

The day was calm and the surface of the sea was quiet and smooth.

"I should say across," I replied. "It will save us a good many miles and there's no danger on a sea like this."

"Straight across it is then", agreed Walter. "It's about a ten hour job, I reckon," and suiting action to his words he bent to his oars and I aided with a paddle.

For an hour we labored and had gotten three or four miles offshore when Walter's oars began to churn up muddy water and all at once the boat stuck fast.

"On a mud bank," growled Walter. "Now isn't that a fix?"

I prodded with my paddle.

"There's hardly a foot of water here. Wait a minute, I'll put on my boots and see if I can find deep water anywhere," I offered.

I pulled on my hip boots and getting overboard waded out around the boat. I even went twenty or thirty rods in either direction with no better results.

"Tell you what it is, Walter," I said. "I remember now that all the steamboats keep close to shore on account of this shoal water out here, and another thing there is some tide even in this extreme end of the Bering Sea."

"That's it then" said Walter. "We might as well take a nap and wait until the tide turns."

Walter actually did fix himself a place on the baggage and dropped off to sleep. I could not quite do that, so I had a lonesome wait of a number of hours and had nothing to do but occasionally test the depth of the water to see if there was any perceptible change. Finally, about four o'clock, I could no-

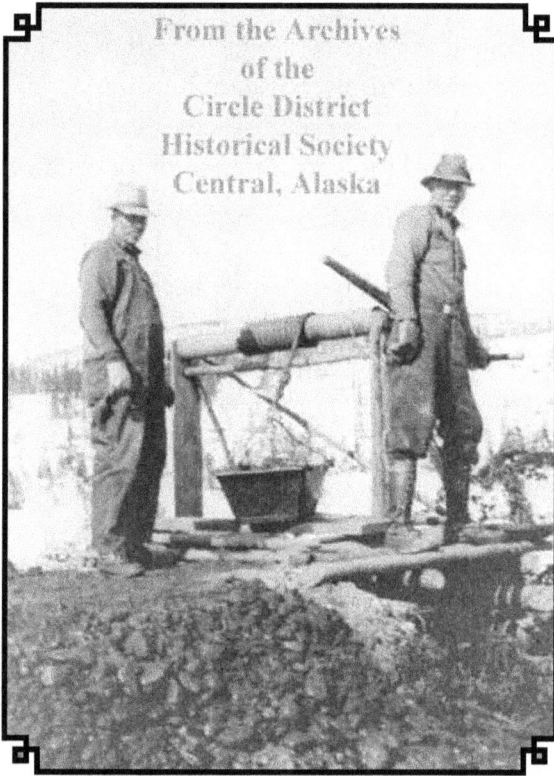

From the Archives
of the
Circle District
Historical Society
Central, Alaska

Working the windlass to bring up materials for dump.

tice an increasing depth, so rousing Walter we both put on our boots and by pushing and pulling began to work the boat toward shore. After a couple of miles had been covered, the boat rode free and we climbed aboard and used our oars. It was too late in the day to round Romanzof that night. There were ten miles of rocky bluffs around the point and it would be no joke to bump into a reef at night.

We made camp on a swampy willow bank. The mosquitoes were fierce and we kept a smudge going to keep the pests down. It is always a question which is worse – the mosquitoes or the dense stifling smoke! The mosquitoes are the torment and pest of all northern countries. The thousands of acres of swamps and tundra, with the ever-pervading moss and lichens affords breeding ground for countless myriads of them. The air becomes thick with them, the sun is even darkened at times, while the vibration of their wings in insurmountable swarms creates a steady, constant murmur.

Life for six weeks in the early summer becomes a burden. Ordinarily, one is obliged to protect one's face with a net made of cheesecloth closely tied around at the neck. Gloves protect one's hands, and it is necessary to sleep under a net of muslin, or try to, for no net yet devised succeeded in keeping out all the venomous brood. Men have even been known to go crazy through loss of sleep and irritation caused by the pests, and it has been reported that bears are even killed by them, the mosquitoes attacking bruin's eyes so that in his attempts to free himself from his tormentors he sometimes blinds himself, and then death from starvation follow. The moose seek the lakes and rivers and immerse their bodies in the water. The Indians, who have been out hunting all the spring, seek areas along the banks of the Yukon where a breeze helps to make life more endurable as it tends to blow the insects away.

We slept but little that night, and by three o'clock the next morning were off for our final drive. After rounding Romanzof, there is an inland channel suitable for small boats which leads into the rear of the seaport and for this we headed. Another long, hard day and we camped on the beach of this volcanic island of St. Michael. Here were headquarters of several trading companies, numerous houses and stores. A fleet of Eskimo bidarkas were drawn upon the beach and several ocean-going steamers were riding at anchor a short distance off shore. There were also numerous miners' and prospectors' boats similar to the one we had been using. Half a dozen men came sauntering down to the beach seeing us pull up in our boat.

"Well, well, look who is here!" sang out a familiar voice.

Oh joy, it was Oliver Torrance and there was Tom Brown's grinning face just beside him! It seems that the two had joined the Dawson rush to Nome, coming down in a small boat, and arriving two days ahead of us! Inquiring, I learned that the boys had worked a leased claim on Gay Gulch the previous winter, making small wages only, so the appeal of the rich Nome beach diggings had drawn them down river with the rest of us.

A large ocean steamer was loading for Nome, distance of which was eighty miles, and took us all, bag and baggage, for $20.00 per person. It was to sail in the morning. The eighty miles was to cross Norton Sound. A few hardy

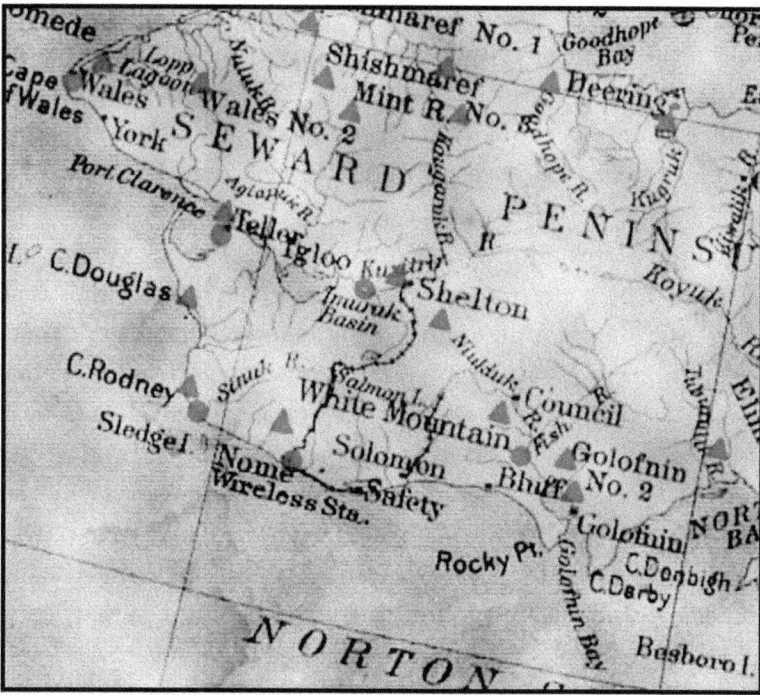

Nome area.

men elected to skirt the coast in their small boats, the distance being double that of the direct course taken by our steamer. The water is shoal off Nome and ocean boats have to anchor three miles out, passengers and freight being towed to shore on barges. A heavy surf was rising and everyone got well sprayed with salt water on making the landing.

A more dreary, desolate place to locate a city could not be imagined! There was not a tree in sight, and nothing but a flat, swamp tundra stretched back for five miles to the low, barren hills of Anvil Creek. The town huddled on the edge of the tundra just back from high water (as was supposed) though later it was found that was not so and some unpredictable high tides damaged and washed away some of the buildings. Gold had been found on Anvil Creek two years before by some men herding the reindeer brought over by the government for the Eskimos. Since the creek proved quite rich with gold, several of the commercial companies build trading posts on the beach. It was while sinking posts for the foundations for one of the buildings that gold was turned up and the famous beach rush was on. By shoveling up the coarse beach sand, a layer of heavy black sand was exposed. This had been beaten up by the waves and in some places proved to be very rich, and, it was felt, there was pay for a distance of twenty miles.

Under United States mining laws, the beach back as far as high tide could not be acquired by a person, so it was a merry scramble, first come, first served; however, the men themselves adopted a tacit agreement that no one should be disturbed in any actual ground he was working. Before fall of that season it was estimated that twenty thousand people were on the beach at or near Nome, digging for riches! It was largely a city of tents and as by the end of the season most of the beach had been worked over, the population faded away as rapidly as it came.

We visited Anvil Creek, a fairly rich placer area, where men were busy sluicing. We met many old acquaintances. Of course, everything even to the mountain tops had been staked. There was nothing for us here unless we chose to go to work for wages. There was talk of new strikes on the Kougarok, a large stream emptying into the sea some seventy-five or one hundred miles farther up the coast near the Bering Strait.

"Let's go," said Walter. Tom and Ollie were agreeable and picking up Jim Bullard, another of my former Circle City friends, we left with our two boats. All this coast is lashed by heavy breakers even in the calmest weather, and at this season of the year there was constant northwest wind. We had to tow our boats all the way up the coast! A bridle was attached to our boat. This consisted of one line hitched to the bow, a second line one third way back to the side, and the two lines joined at the tow line. If the attachment is just right, the boat will ride along parallel to the shore without being drawn to land. One man had to ride in the boat to see that it kept clear of the outer line of the surf. He had a cold, sometimes wet job, and was very glad when the time came to shift to the tow line. If one has dogs they can be hitched to the tow lines, but we had left our dogs at Weare.

It took a week to work (and that is the correct word) up the coast to Port Clarence. Here is a large land-locked saltwater by and opening into that a chain of quite large lakes, one feeding into the other. These were fed by the

Kougarok and other streams. As this chain of lakes led nearly due east, we could use our head wind, now a quartering one, so improvising sails we made much better and easier time. There was nothing but swamp willow for fuel and it was green at that. I sighed for the good birch and spruce of the Tanana. At the head of the last lake tundra began, nothing but tundra, miles of it! But across it loomed the mountains of the Kougarok and across the dreary waste we toiled. These were high, bold mountains of magnesium limestone, not gold-bearing in themselves, but they had been capped in the ages past with schist and shale that were gold-bearing. These latter now had been largely worn away depositing what gold they had carried in the beds of the streams. It was these streams that we panned, but all proved to contain low grade pay, no better in fact, nor as good, as those streams we had on the Chena.

"What a horrible country to winter in," commented Ollie, and so said all of us.

Back to Nome we went to get our mail, and to get passage on an ocean steamer again. We made much better time on the return trip as we had a wind in our back and the two ropes were dispensed with. The ocean steamer had arrived, bringing not only mail but also thousands of adventurers. Brown, Bullard, and Watson decided to go to work in the mines on Anvil Creek and at the close of the year to go outside.

"I go up to Dawson," I declared.

"I'll go with you," said Torrance, "and put in one more year in this country."

We walked over to Anvil to see the boys before we left for up river. Little did we, or anyone else, dream as we tramped through the marshy tundra that we were trudging over millions of dollars of gold, but so it was and a few years later three ancient ocean beaches were located between the first original beach and the foothills of Anvil. The last of these three beaches proved to be enormously rich and fortunes were taken from it. However, it was not for us and bidding good-by to the other boys, Ollie and I shipped on a riverboat for Dawson in the Klondike regions of Canada, reaching that place just before the river froze up for the season.

Chapter 29
Dawson
Winter, 1900 & Spring, 1901

Both Ollie and I were at the end of our resources and we must speedily find some way of getting money as it was expensive living in the North in those days. It was my first time in Dawson. I had drifted past its location seven years before on my way to Forty Mile when then only existed a barren river flat much like hundreds of others up and down the river. With the discovery of the rich placer bars on Bonanza and Eldorado Creeks, a thriving city of ten or twelve thousand people came into existence and at this time with the gold pouring in from the nearby mines, a flourishing business was carried on.

Our first thoughts were to check out the mines and we made a trip out to Bonanza and the other rich streams. We would much have preferred a lease and to work it ourselves, but at that late date nothing that interested us was presented. Then I ran across an old Circle City acquaintance, Jack Nelson. He was a foreman or manager for Joe Burke, one of the Dawson merchants who owned a good claim on Upper Bonanza. Jack at once asked me to come and work for him.

"You are just the man I need," he declared. "I am going to drift this winter and want to start in right away getting ready for it. You know all about machinery. I need you to help set up the boiler, build a hoist, and make a set of steam heads for thawing. The wages are a dollar an hour and board and lodging. You can put in as much overtime as you wish. What do you say?"

It was a remarkably good offer and I closed the deal for it at once. I introduced Ollie to Jack, and Jack promised him work as soon as we got the machinery ready for production. Thawing by steam was an innovation that had just come in vogue in Dawson. Instead of the slow and disagreeable and many times dangerous method we had used in Circle City of thawing by means of wood fires, steam from a boiler, on the surface of the ground, was carried underground and used to thaw the frozen gravel and bedrock. A section of hydraulic steel pipe was given a strong point in which was an orifice not much larger than a knitting needle. The other end of the pipe had a solid iron head. A nipple just below this entered the pipe and the nipple was connected to a rubber hose with the steam pipe from the boiler. A set of twelve points made up a "head." The pipes were from six feet to twelve feet long. When ready to operate, the points were arranged on the floor of the drift ten and one half feet apart. They were entered in the frozen ground just on top of bedrock as the driving was easier there, no large rock or boulder being in the way to block the driving. Steam was then turned on. It took two men to operate the drive. With the first hiss of steam against the ground, gravel and rocks were sent flying. A blow from a sledge hammer would send the point into the frozen mass a foot. Another blow and another foot was gained. Meantime the next point was placed ready and that was started in a similar manner, and so on until the whole set had been entered. Then one after the other all the points were driven in until all were flush with the face of the drift. Steam was now kept on for ten or twelve hours, usually all night until the day crew came to work in the morning. This portion of the work was looked after by the men firing the boiler. An occasional visit to the drift was necessary to see that everything was working correctly.

In the morning, the points were removed and the now warm and steaming mass that had been thawed was allowed to remain for three days before being removed. If the job had been successful, there was now a well thawed body of gravel and bedrock six feet high, thirty feet wide, and twelve or more feet in depth depending on the length of the points used. The next night the set was moved to one side of the former thaw and the process repeated, and so on in succession, the aim being to keep three days material ahead of the men. It was so much faster, cleaner, and healthier than the old wood burning method.

I was glad to be able to get the job of getting all the machinery ready for the operation. I rigged up a fifty foot gin pole and the buckets from the mine shaft were run on a wire cable to the top of the pole and would dump by a mechanical device. Our aim was twelve hundred buckets per day, each holding half a cubic yard of gravel. When all this was ready, Jack called in a dozen men, including Torrance, and a busy winter ensued. Soon we had a regular mountain of pay dirt looming up. This, of course, would have to be reshoveled into sluice boxes in the spring. Meanwhile, another holiday season came and went, and it was 1902.

Soon after Christmas, another old Circle City and Forty Mile pal arrived. This was George Friend, and he was to be associated with me all the remaining time I was in the northland. George was a Virginian and had been in Alaska even more years than I. He was a sourdough of all sourdoughs. He had mushed the trails driving dog teams, had prospected, had mined, had gone hungry, been shipwrecked, made money and lost money, in fact, he had gone through all the varied experiences of a roving life. He had many friends in every camp and, what was better, he lived up to his name and never went back on a friend! Of course, Jack and I were glad to see George. He and I had many a long talk over the years we had known each other. Jack immediately hired him to assist us.

When spring came, we sluiced the mountain of pay dirt we had taken out, and then I fixed up a mud box and we dumped the thawed dirt from the mine directly into the mud box and sluices so saving an extra handling. This work continued until the end of July when the mine had to be closed down until the following winter.

Eight months work at a dollar an hour, many days of fifteen hours, and with no expense for meals or lodging had netted me quite a neat sum and I sent a few thousand dollars out to my wife and children.

Ollie felt he must go home, so we saw him off with a goodly amount of gold in his poke. I would stay on in Dawson.

Chapter 30

George and I Take a Pack Trip

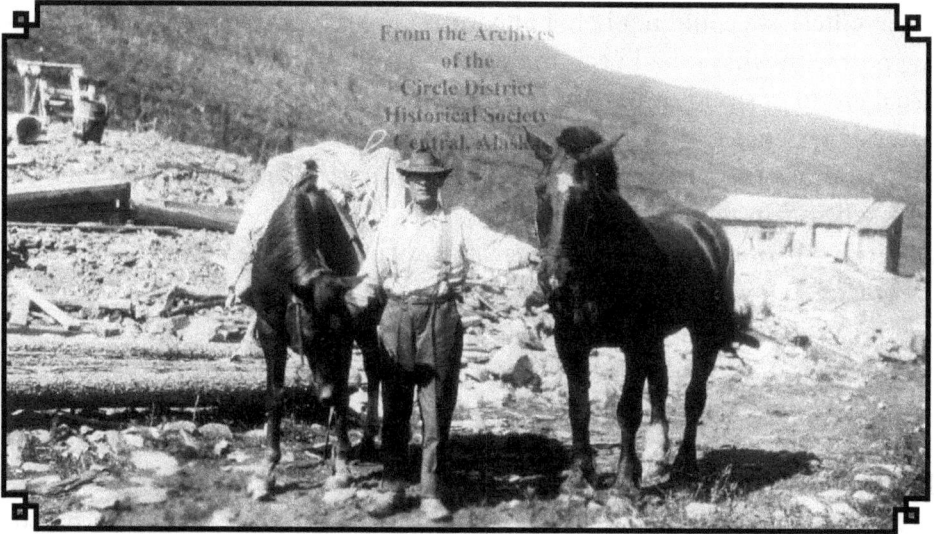

Prospector with horses.

During the winter I had frequently talked with George and Joe Burke, the owner of the mine, about the Chena and Tanana region. At the time the mine closed down, some men from the outside arrived in Dawson with a band of broncos from Oregon.

One day George surprised me by saying, "Fred, let's buy two or three of those broncos and take a trip over into that country of yours – we need a vacation and it will be three months before there is any more work here. What do you say?"

The idea appealed to me. Going into Dawson and telling Joe Burke of our plans, he fell in with the idea and asked to be in on it too. He offered to put up $500 for a grubstake for me, and Doc Roan put up $500 grubstake for George, and they asked we be four equal partners in anything we might find. We agreed. We purchased three of the animals, a black, a bay and a small white one for three hundred dollars each. I presume the nags had not cost over ten or twelve dollars apiece outside, but we could not argue the price. The animals had to be shod and pack saddles purchased, and an outfit for three months provided. We were given pointers on throwing the diamond hitch, and we soon caught the trick of it.

An A.C. boat was leaving for the lower river and we shipped our outfit to Circle City, a good starting point for our overland trip, we thought. Unloading at Circle, we could not help but contrast the present almost deserted trading post with what it had been in the boom days of '94 to '96. There was the usual group of stolid Indians watching us unload the animals and our outfit. Several of them we knew from former acquaintance, among them was Alga, a rather notorious Indian woman. She was evidently a disciple of Ben Lindsey and believed in companionate associations, changing her place of abode as the grub pile of her temporary "husband" dwindled.

I greeted her with, "Hello, Alga. How are you getting along?"

"Oh," she replied, "have you heard of our trouble?"

"Why no, Alga, what trouble have you had?"

"Well, we had to get married!" she replied.

It seems Uncle Sam had just issued an edict that any white man living with an Indian woman must marry her or give her up. Hence Alga's trouble arrived!

We did not tarry long in Circle, but packing our outfit on our animals we started over the familiar trail to the Junction and Hoggum. The bay we had named Buck because of the exhibition he always gave, and the Indians were much amused by him. Buck usually repeated the performance every morning upon being loaded up, but the other two, Black and Whitey, were very docile and gave us no trouble.

The old trail was quite familiar to us although we formerly had usually travelled it in the winter time with dog teams. Crossing the tundra was tedious and the swarms of mosquitoes were hovering over us and the animals in dense clouds. They were especially bad on Blackie, much worse than on either of the other two animals, but why we did not know.

That night we made Hoggum, where we found some fairly good grass for the horses. Our plan at first was to picket one of the animals, letting the other two run loose. Later, we found we could turn all three of them out to forage for themselves. We found a few men at work along the creek but the most part of it had been gone over and over and abandoned.

The next day took us up over the divide at the head of Hoggum into a new and unknown country. From the top of the divide we got a good view. Away off north, east, and south, rose one range of mountains after another, seemingly a jumbled mass of peaks. Somewhere southeast, a hundred and fifty miles away lay the Chena and our destination.

"How in the world will you ever find the Chena, Fred?" asked George. "One peak and one range of mountains look just like another, and you have never been over this part of the country before."

"Well, George," I replied, "it may seem queer to you, but there is something in my head that just seems to pull me in the right direction. I have always had it and I never lose my way."

That was not boasting, for some people are so constructed that they rarely get lost. I used to say they have a "bump of location." Poor Pedro lacked that quality or he would never have lost his pay creek!

We took things leisurely, going only fifteen or twenty miles a day, giving the horses plenty of time to graze. Some nights when the mosquitoes were unusually bad, the horses refused to stay in the open but hunted a dense patch of willows where they could weave around through the brush, freeing themselves from their tormentors. Consequently, their only provender on such nights was the browse from the willow tips. We got to building smudges for them and they learned to hover in the dense smoke. Little Whitey would hardly leave the campfire and teased for bits of bread from our table.

We crossed many streams, all of them we presumed to be tributaries of Birch Creek. The tenth night out we camped on a small creek running toward the southeast.

"George," I said, "when we top that divide tomorrow we will look down on my old cabin on the Chena!"

"Bet you a hundred dollars we won't" he challenged. "You are lost and I know it!"

But I was right! When we gained the top in the morning, there were our little cabins nestled together in the little open clearing just as I had left them two years before. It seemed like home to pull the latch string and push open the door of the one I claimed as mine. A somewhat damp and musty odor greeted us, but everything was in good order. There in a bookshelf was the year's copy of the "Outlook" and several books we had left. A note on the table told how three trappers had used the cabin the previous winter and how much they had enjoyed the library. We spent several days at the camp resting the horses and ourselves.

The salmon were busy on the spawning beds, and we enjoyed a few meals of fresh salmon. Usually our fish diet had consisted of grayling. When we had camped at nights, George would start a fire and make preparations for a meal while I took my pole and line and cast for grayling. They were eager for the fly and I usually had a dozen in short order. I kept only those weighing half a pound or less, as a three pounder was too large for our frying pans. I remember one evening I hooked and landed a three pounder twice in succession. It was the same fish each time as I could see by his torn lip!

From the cabins we had almost ten miles of river to go before reaching the mouth of the Black Shale. Here I showed George where I had got a dollar a pan on bedrock and some favorable prospects in gravel. We looked the ground over pretty thoroughly and decided that the prospect warranted taking a chance on it. The big body of gravel on the main Chena would be a dredging project. We staked five miles of the creek using "power of attorney" that we had brought with us. Of course, there was nothing we could do this late in the summer, but we planned to return the following winter with an outfit.

The next day we climbed the divide and crossed over onto the Saltchocket. We ran into a rough granite barrier that crossed the divide. Here above this granite we saw a huge body of quartz-carrying galena ore. We followed down Saltchocket about twenty miles, but found nothing that interested us so made a long swing back over the divide dropping down into the north fork of the Chena about ten miles below our cabins. Pannings on this creek showed it to be gold bearing. I got one pan of four or five cents and another of eight cents on the rim in one place. We decided to remember this creek and possibly do some prospecting on it when we returned in the winter. We could now retrace our steps to Circle or, as I suggested, go across a couple of ranges farther north and get onto creeks heading against Baker Creek.

While we were eating lunch, there came up one of those sudden thunderstorms so frequent in Alaska late summer and early fall. There was not much rain, but a sudden bolt of lightening struck a dry stub of spruce just over against our camp. The bolt set the stub on fire. It continued to burn all that afternoon and by evening had got a good hold in the half-dry moss and peat that covered the land like a blanket. The growing trees, loaded with their weight of cones and pitch, caught fire and soon the whole countryside was a ranging inferno. We had to move out and two days later as we topped the divide on the far side of the Chena, I looked back and could still see the pall of smoke hanging on the horizon twenty miles south of us.

These fires, mainly caused by natural causes similar to the one we had just witnessed, were a constant source of interest to me. The country, with the exception of the bare ridges and divides, was covered with a thick carpet of moss and peat. As this heavy layer prevents the short summer season from thawing the underlying soil, there is nothing in the tree line that will grow in the moss but the white spruce. It is shallow-rooted and sends out long feelers just between the moss and the top soil. When a disastrous fire such as the one we had just seen occurred, the moss and peat burn off. The trees are left blackened, and limbless trunks standing on the burned-off surface are ready to topple over with the first wind. Now nature takes her turn. On this burned over tract springs up a crop of wild Alaskan red top. I remember one spot a short distance above our cabins on the Chena where a meadow, ten thousand acres in extent, was covered with red top growing higher than my head. All through it were the fallen spruces, some of them two feet in diameter, and when a mass of these fallen trees had choked down the red top, there were great, luscious red raspberries and in other openings blueberries abounded. In the course of the years, how many I could only guess, poplars and the white paper birch would take the place of the red top. These poplar and birch thickets were great winter homes for the moose. As more years pass and the ever prevailing moss is once more covering the ground, killing the birch and the poplar, then the last of the cycle comes bringing the spruce. On our trip we saw several of these fire scars in all stages of transition.

Crossing a rather difficult divide on the north side of the Chena, we dropped down into a valley that was thickly clothed with birch and poplar. Evidently this stream was a tributary of the Chena and probably was that fork of the river that we had noticed when we first started up the latter stream. We saw a bear eating blueberries and watched him for several minutes. We came to another divide. We could trace this one stretching away toward the Tanana River. From our vantage point on this divide, we got a comprehensive outlook over a vast extent of the country. Away toward the north were high snow-white peaks, evidently a main divide between the waters of the Yukon and the Tanana system. Between us and that high divide was a network of streams leading in an easterly direction to the Tanana. The stream at our feet was either the Tolovana or one of its main tributaries. It was the "great un-known" of our Circle City days.

On descending into the valley, we saw traces of previous prospectors and some abandoned workings. There was no one on the gulch until near a fork we encountered "Old Slade." He told us all the men had gone to Circle for supplies. There had been some pay taken out that summer, but the development work was only beginning and no one could say whether the creek would prove to be good or not. According to "Old Slade", it was about twenty miles up the creek to its head against Miller Creek. It was already late September and the nights were getting cold. Soon there would be snow on the ground.

"Let's head for home," said George. "We'll buy our winter outfit in Circle, make arrangements to have it freighted to Hoggum where we will pick it up next winter."

Starting out on the last lap of our trip we ran into a band of caribou.

"Why not pack in a load of fresh meat to Circle?" asked George. "There will always be a demand for meat there and we might as well make a little money out of our horses."

We shot four caribou and packed the meat, two carcasses apiece on Buck and Black, leaving Whitey to carry our packs and camp equipment, now reduced to bedding and only a few supplies. Miller Creek was next to and parallel to Mastodon on which I had mined. We found one or two men still on Miller, though the work had closed down for the season. The creek was a short one, only about six miles long. These three creeks, Miller, Mastodon, and Independence, all dumped their water into the larger Mammoth Creek. Here, just below the mouth of the last one of the creeks, was Henry Lewis. He had staked a lot of claims and was waiting for a dredging outfit to take up and develop the property. No doubt it has since been done. We spent the night with Henry, then went on to Circle City, over now familiar ground. In Circle City we recorded the claims we had located on Black Shale.

We found a ready sale for our caribou meat, but when it came to disposing of our animals it was not so easy. The price of hay in Dawson had been $400 a ton, and an animal would eat two tons throughout the winter. That, of course, was prohibitive and besides we would have no use for horses. At last a freighter with dog teams offered us $100 for the three animals. He told us frankly he would have to kill the horses and use the meat to feed his dogs. There seemed nothing else to do, so we had to let them go at that price which would just pay the cost of freighting an outfit to Big Louis's cabin on Hoggum.

Chapter 31

Dominion #7 Above, Lower Creek

Winter, 1902

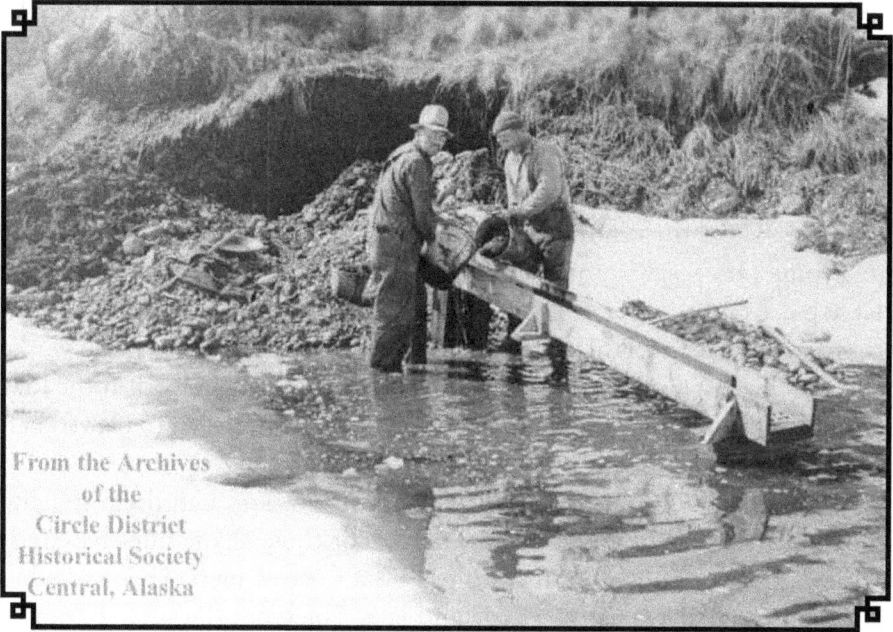

From the Archives
of the
Circle District
Historical Society
Central, Alaska

Two men spring sluicing at hillside cut.

The *P.B. Weare* arrived in Circle and we boarded it and got back to Dawson two days later. We had been gone nearly three months. We met with Joe Burke and Doc Roan and talked over our trip.

"Drop it for now, boys," suggested Joe. "You may have something out there, and again you may not. We can always check it out later. Meanwhile, I have a proposition that is a sure thing and I think a very good thing too. You know, I have a claim on Dominion Creek, No. 7 Above, Lower Creek. Well, the man, Old Stone, who has had a lease on it has struck it rich and I learn he has been stealing from me, so I have cancelled his lease. You go over there and take the lease over. I will give you 70% of what you take out and I will go good for all your expenses at any of the Dawson stores. Think it over."

George and I talked it over.

"Let's run out to Dominion, George," I suggested, "and look the ground over first."

"All right," replied George.

Dominion Creek headed against the rich Bonanza where we had worked the past winter, so the trail to Dominion was familiar to us. We simply had to cross a low divide between the two streams. All along the creek for ten or fifteen miles were cabins and open cuts showing busy workings. Many rich strikes had been made and the pay streak was wide and promised to hold out well. We had no trouble in locating No. 7 Above, Lower. On it we found a very comfortable cabin and, in fact, Mr. Stone, the man we were to dispossess. He was very frank about the matter, said he had some disagreement with Joe Burke so had thrown up the lease. However, he acknowledged he had located some very good pay and would give us all the help he could. There was a large piece on the lower end of the ground that had never been worked, and Mr. Stone informed us that the owners of the claim below No. 7 had worked up to the line last winter in good pay. He advised starting in work at the lower line. The outlook seemed good to both of us, and we returned to Dawson and closed the agreement with Burke.

Next, we bought an outfit of tools and provisions and had them freighted over to our claim. We proposed to sink two or three shafts ourselves and if we located good enough pay dirt, to put on a force of men. That was a busy fall for both of us. We worked early and late. The ground was deep, not less than twenty feet, and on one side it was thirty. It was the old grind of build a fire, let it thaw at night, shovel it out the next day and then build another fire. We started all three shafts at the same time. After the shafts got too deep to shovel out, we had to put up a windlass and rig a rope and bucket to hoist the thawed material. That took two of us, one on top, generally myself, and George below. As the shafts neared bedrock, we also had to do a lot of panning. The first two shafts showed good pay but nothing extraordinarily rich. It was in the third shaft, near the lower line, that one evening as I hoisted the last bucket of the day, I saw several specks of yellow material.

"This dirt looks good, George," I called down. "I can see gold all through it!"

"Try a pan," suggested my partner.

I did so and announced triumphantly, "There's ten dollars if there's a cent!"

"Plenty more just like it down here," called up George.

The prospect certainly did look good.

"We'll put some men at work and if it shows up as well as the prospects do, we'll make old Joe fit us out with some machinery and make a killing this winter," declared George.

We hired a man to deliver one thousand dollars' worth of wood which was to be used largely for thawing underground. Next, we hired twelve men and opened up two shafts, in fact sinking two more fifty feet above these latter ones. It kept me busy testing the dirt as it was taken out. The third shaft still proved to be the richest one and, in fact, in drifting we struck still richer dirt, several pans showing over one hundred dollars. One day one of the men handed George a nugget of gold worth forty dollars.

I have sometimes been asked if the men did not steal the gold when they were working in such rich diggings. I expect the temptation to do so was more than some of them could resist. However, we placed no restrictions on the men and as George said, "What we don't know they steal won't hurt us."

After working a month, we had a good body of pay ore opened up and we decided to see Joe Burke about some machinery. We would need a boiler, several hundred feet of iron pipe, three sets of hydraulic points and a steam pump and hoist. That would run into several thousand dollars. Joe Burke rather hesitated.

"You know, boys," he said, "in this country you are under Canadian laws. If you go in debt and can't pay your bills they will not let you leave the country, and if you try to, the officials will put you in jail. Better go slow."

"But we've got the pay, Joe," George replied, "and we are willing to risk jail!"

"All right, you shall have the machinery as soon as I can ship it out. Both of you men have had experience enough to know what you are talking about."

Back we went to Dominion and made preparations for installing the machinery. We had to build a log cabin to house the boiler. I also rigged up a saw to cut up the wood into short lengths for the furnace, and concocted a hoist. I cut up and made the heads for the steam points, installed the pump into the drift when it arrived. George was everywhere. He kept the men at work while the preparation for the machinery was going on and helped me when he could. Up to this time we had been boarding the men, but it took up too much of my time to do cooking for so many, so we engaged board both for the men and ourselves at a nearby lodging house run by the Shropshire Brothers.

Chapter 32
Gold-Filled Mammoth Teeth

Before Christmas time, 1902, we had everything running in good condition and were taking out dirt in great quantities. One day one of the men came up and said they had found the skeleton of a mammoth and also a bison down on bedrock about twenty feet from the surface. I went down into the drift to see the find. The men were pulling and tugging at the bones. The heavy tusks took two men to lift. The tusks were cracked and broken, not near as fine a pair as some I had seen. However, I saved some of the molars, several of which weighed 16 pounds apiece. Each was quite well preserved.

"Whoever heard of a mammoth having gold-filled teeth!" exclaimed George as he picked out small pieces of gold from the roots of the teeth. In fact, these latter had acted as riffles collecting small particles of gold as the ancient streams had washed it around them. I carried some of these teeth home with me in my suitcase and for years afterwards every time they were dusted, small flecks of gold would fall out of them! They were quite conversation pieces.

About this time an unusually cold spell of weather set it, and the thermometer registered from 56 degrees to 67 degrees below for ten days. It was rather severe on the two men above ground who had to tend the hoist and dump the gravel. I offered to knock off work for the time being, fearing for the health of the outside men, but they wouldn't listen to my offer.

"We don't mind the cold," they claimed.

The men underground were as comfortable as ever. They worked in their shirtsleeves, but I noticed the minute they got above ground they donned their parkas and made a run for the bunkhouse!

One day one of the boys by mistake turned off the steam in the pipe running to the pump and forgot to drain the latter. The error lasted for but half an hour, but it was long enough to cause the water in the pipe and pump to congeal and burst the pump head and nearly one hundred feet of pipe. We had to send the pump head into Dawson for repairs and install a new pipe. I had to make a run into the town too, to see about some matters pertaining to the mine, so made the trip with our dogs. Climbing up out of Dominion, I struck the stage road leading down into Bonanza. It had been graded during the summer and was now a well-packed snow trail with a gradual incline of five miles down to the workings on Bonanza. It looked from the top like an ideal coasting run, so I turned the dogs loose and took a coast. It was magnificent! The grade was not steep enough to make the speed dangerous, but it kept the dogs going at top speed to keep up with me and how they ki-kied if the sled gained on them. They enjoyed the run as much as I did and we all reached the bottom of the grade at the same time. The dogs panting and blowing. I gave the dogs a short rest to recover their breath and we made the remainder of the twenty miles into Dawson.

At this time Dawson was a gay city. It was right at the height of its bonanza years. Electric lights had been installed, a water system where steam was injected in the water pipes to keep the latter from bursting was also being used. There was a school, several churches, and a Sisters' Hospital. All the main street was a line of saloons, gambling houses, dance halls, and all night one could hear the calls of the croupiers at the gaming tables where thousands of dollars in dust changed hands nightly. The Canadian mounted police had barracks in the city and law and order for such a frontier mining camp was well maintained. Of course, there were occasional shootings and murders, but the police "got their man" and the better element of society backed them up.

I visited the school one day and it did seem odd to see the teacher light lanterns for the little ones and send them home at three o'clock in the afternoon, and to watch the kiddies go bobbing along the snow trails to their homes like so many little fireflies like I used to see in the summer evenings in my boyhood home in Wisconsin.

I returned to Dominion for Christmas, 1902, and after that holiday returned to a steady grind of work. I turned over to one of the men the running of the hoist and devoted most of my time to directing the work underground in the daytime, while George took on the night shift. We lost no more time during the rest of the winter.

Chapter 33
We Weather a Labor Strike
Spring, 1903

Boiler House on Little El Dorado Creek.

January, February, March of 1903 passed and April brought longer and longer hours of sunlight. We expected water would be running in the creek by the middle, or at latest, twenty-fifth of May. I now ordered lumber for sluice boxes, also a small centrifugal pump to raise water from the creek when the sluicing season opened. It kept me busy making the boxes and getting everything ready. It kept me busy making the boxes and getting everything ready. We had one of the dumps of pay dirt directly on the ice of the frozen creek, a rather risky thing to do for if the first water should come with a flood, we might lose the whole dump! I got all the string of boxes set up, the pump installed, and connected by a long time of six inch canvas hose to the head sluice box. On the seventh of May a light stream of water began to trickle down the creek.

"Is everything ready for tomorrow?" asked George that evening. "I think there will be water enough to start a run by ten o'clock."

"Everything is o.k., George," I replied.

An hour later, one of the men came into room and asked to see me. He appeared rather uneasy and stood twirling his cap in his hands.

"What is it, Dick?" I asked.

"Say, you going to start shoveling in tomorrow?" he asked.

"Yes, Dick, if there is water enough to fill the boxes we will start," I answered.

"Well, the men sent me in to tell you we want a raise in pay, want two dollars and a half more per day."

"But Dick, we have paid you the highest wages on the gulch all winter, and boarded you too! Why should we pay this extra amount now?" I asked.

"You've had good dirt all winter long and you can afford the raise," continued Dick, "besides, that dump on the ice will all be lost if we strike as we have agreed to do if you do not come through with the raise!"

"That's your ultimatum, is it?" I asked.

"You bet it is," Dick answered.

Just then George came into the room and I said to him, "George, see here is Dick with a demand from the men for a raise of two fifty per day or they strike!"

"What!" shouted George. "The dirty dogs. Think they have us in a hole and trying to take advantage of us that way after the good treatment we have given them this winter!"

"They say we will lose that dump on the ice," I calmly replied.

"To hell with the dump!" yelled my partner. "I'd rather lose all the other dumps too then be held up this way! I tell you what, Fred, you pay off every last one of them this evening and fire them all. See that they leave the claim first thing in the morning. I'll see what I can do." He opened the door and disappeared into the darkness.

"Call the other men in, Dick, and I will make out all their time," I directed.

The men filed in and I paid off each man in currency I had borrowed from Joe Burke a few days previously. The men took their money silently and filed out. I think they were taken by surprise both by the fact that I had the money on hand to pay them and that we took the prospective loss of the dump on the ice so quietly! About midnight George came in and was in great good humor.

"Have you settled with the bunch?" he asked immediately.

"Yes, George, they are all paid and they leave the claim in the morning," I answered.

"Good! I went down to see the men on the claim below us and told them what we were up against. They are going to send a crew up here and shovel in that creek dump for us, then we can get a new crew in from Dawson for the rest of the work."

By ten o'clock the water had started running and the crew went to work. I saw our former men starting off with their packs on their backs, rather a sorry and crestfallen crowd. In fact, I heard later that no one on the gulch would give them any work all summer long. The dump was not a very large one and by nightfall we saw the last shovelful running through the boxes. George and I "cleaned up" by moonlight about ten thousand dollars!

There was no trouble in getting a new crew of men to replace the old one, and the remainder of the winter and spring work was soon safely sluiced. We settled with Burke for his percentage of the cleanup, then paid all our debts for machinery, wood and other things and had a tidy nest egg left for ourselves.

The summer work was similar to that of the winter except that the thawed dirt was hoisted and dumped directly into the mud box which was simply only a little longer and wider sluice box at the head of the string. As the hoist brought up many large rocks and even boulders that were imbedded in the pay dirt, they had to be washed to save the gold adhering to them. We stationed a man by this mud box to fork out the larger rocks and keep them from clogging up the sluices. The days were long now and warm. There were many summer showers but nothing to prevent working. We had no more "labor" troubles. I made an occasional run to Dawson on business, and those days were the only breaks in a long, continuous summer's work.

Chapter 34
I Return Home
Fall, 1903

Preparations were made for another winter's campaign. We bought three thousand dollars' worth of wood and some additional tools and machinery.

We were getting mail from the outside quite regularly now. The Canadian government had established a fortnightly service down the river so letters from the outside were only a month old. It was quite different from those early years when eighteen months was considered the very earliest one could get a reply to word sent outside, and often the time was even longer.

Before our second winter's work had begun, I received a letter from my mother begging me to come out and help her. My father had died two years previously, my only brother, Harry, had lost his life in the attack on Manilla during the Spanish American War, and mother was left with the care of the old house and needed my help. I talked the matter over with George.

"Go out, certainly," said George. "If it were my mother I wouldn't let anything keep me from going."

"About our lease," I queried. "We have everything ready for a profitable winter's work. If you will run it, George, I will pay half the expenses and share fifty-fifty with you."

"No," replied George. "You have always handled the machinery and done all the bookkeeping. I might make a botch out of that line. I'll tell you what. Old Stone has offered to take over our lease at a profit to us anytime, and buy all the machinery and wood at cost. Stone and Joe Burke seem to have settled their differences by now and are on good terms again and I am sure Joe won't mind letting him have another go at it. So we will sell our lease to him and I will look for something else. Anyway, there is always the claims on the Black Shale to fall back on!"

"That is fine of you, George," said I, "but it lets you out of what is almost sure to be a good winter's work."

"Oh, that is o.k. with me," replied my partner. "You would do the same in my case, I know."

So ended my mining experiences in Alaska and the Klondike. I left in late September, 1903, and boarded the Clifford Sifton, a light up-river steamboat plying between Dawson and Whitehorse, the Yukon terminus of the White Pass and the Yukon Railroad. A sourdough's backtracking I called it. As the boat swung out into the broad stream, I turned for a farewell look at the struggling city where so many dramas had been played. I saw the broad scar on the mountainside where an immense landslide had buried a village of Moosehide Indians. I saw the Ogilvie bridge across the Klondike, the first steel bridge on the Yukon, and lastly I saw the well-beloved form of George Friend waving good-by and good luck to me.

Up the broad reaches of the Yukon crept the Clifford Sifton, past Pelly River, past White River with its milky water caused by the cutting of volcanic ash bluffs laid down long ago by an explosion from Mt. Katmai, past Big and Little Salmon Rivers, through the Five Fingers Rapids where we were drawn by cable, and lastly we tied up at the wharf at Whitehorse, now a thriving village.

The train was waiting for the steamer and but little delay occurred before we were off on the one hundred and forty miles to Skagway and the ocean liner. What a difference ten years had made in the method of transportation! I looked back in memory of the long days of toil, pulling a sled over the icy trails, and the work of whipsawing lumber to build our boats, the treacherous ice where a slip of the foot meant death. In a flashback of memory, I gasped as I broke through a snow bridge into a crevasse, and but for the fact that I was holding my long-handled shovel crosswise to the opening, I would have been plunged into unknown depths in the icy interior and my days brought to an untimely end! It was only six hours by train where it had taken us six weeks back in 1894!

We slid down the switchback into Skagway, the town of Soapy Smith of notorious fame. The train continued out on the mile-long pier to the ocean liner, then there were a few delightful days through the Inland Passage to Puget Sound and Seattle.

I made a visit to the mint where my dust was changed to coin of the realm, then the Northern Pacific Railroad took me eastward and home to wife, children, and relatives. The ten year long adventure in the Northland was ended.

End

Epilogue

The first printing of this book was released to the public on September 7, 2018 at the Morris Thompson Center in Fairbanks, AK. We invited Frederick's grandson (Kirke Currier Jorgensen) to join us for the event. There was a great turn-out. Fairbanks residents were eager to get a copy of the book.

Prior to making the trip to Alaska, Kirke informed us that he would bring other materials related to the book, which he planned to leave with us. At the time, I was so busy that his comments went right in one ear and out the other. However, I was blown away the day after the release party, when Kirke handed over:

- All of the letters that Frederick had mailed to his family during his time in Alaska,
- All of the letters that Frederick had received from his family during his time in Alaska,
- A series of photos not previously seen by anyone in Alaska, and
- The original hand-written manuscript of this book.

To say that it was exciting to accept these materials would be a huge understatement. This was as exciting as the first time I read the manuscript and realized that we had a fabulous book on our hands.

A group of three Fairbanks amateur historians (Dirk Tordoff, George Lounsbury and myself) decided that we would have all of these documents scanned. The originals were subsequently donated to the Archives and the University of Alaska. Copies of the scans were given to the Pioneers of Alaska Igloo #4 in Fairbanks and the Circle District Historical Society's museum in Central.

We greatly thank Kirke and his family for donating these materials. They are important historical documents and as one person pointed, they " ... effectively re-write the early history of the Chena River drainage." They are indeed that valuable.

~ *Randy Zarnke*

Photos from the Currier Expedition

Bear killed on Saltito River. 1900

Tents on the North Fork of the Chena Rive
Enroute from steamboats to Fort Independenc
189

Granite Crag with Reindeer moss in foreground.

Currier's dog, Bella. Note saw pit to left

Fred Currier and a moose skin.
Fort Independence, 1899

Tom Brown and Ed Cochran skinning a caribou at head of North Fork of Chena River. 1898

Fort Independence with Oliver Torrence,
Ed Conrad, Tom Brown, Charles Bliss,
Fred Currier, Dingo and Bella.

	NAME	DATE OF LOCATING IN ALASKA.		POST-OFFICE ADDRESS AT HOME.	RELATION.	PERSONAL DESCRIPTION.				DATE OF BIRTH.		
Number of family in the order of visitation.	of each person whose place of abode is in this family or dwelling. Surname first, Christian name in full, and initial. Include every person living on June 1, 1900. Omit children born since June 1, 1900.	Month.	Year.		Relationship of each person to the head of the family.	Color.	Sex.	Age at last birthday.	Conjugal condition.	Month.	Year.	
3	4	5		6	7	8	9	10	11		12
7	Conrad _____	_____	1898	_____ W.	107	W	M	28	Feb	1862	
	Currie _____ J.	Oct	1894	_____ Falls W.		W	M	40	Feb	1860	
8	Strcouber _____	July	1898	Erie Pa.	107	W	M	47	Aug	1850	Sg
	Helen _____	July	1898	Gloucester Mass		W	M	51	May	1848	Sg
9	Gibbs Frank	July	1898	Taylor Falls Minn	107	W	M	28	Dec	1871	Sg
	Oliver _____	July	1898	Taylor Falls Minn		W	M	28	Sep	1871	Sg
	Here ends the enumeration of Ft. Independence										

Census from Fort Independence. 1898

A VERY dedicated census worker traveled to the upper Chena in 1900 to gather data on the Currier party. These are copies of the original forms.

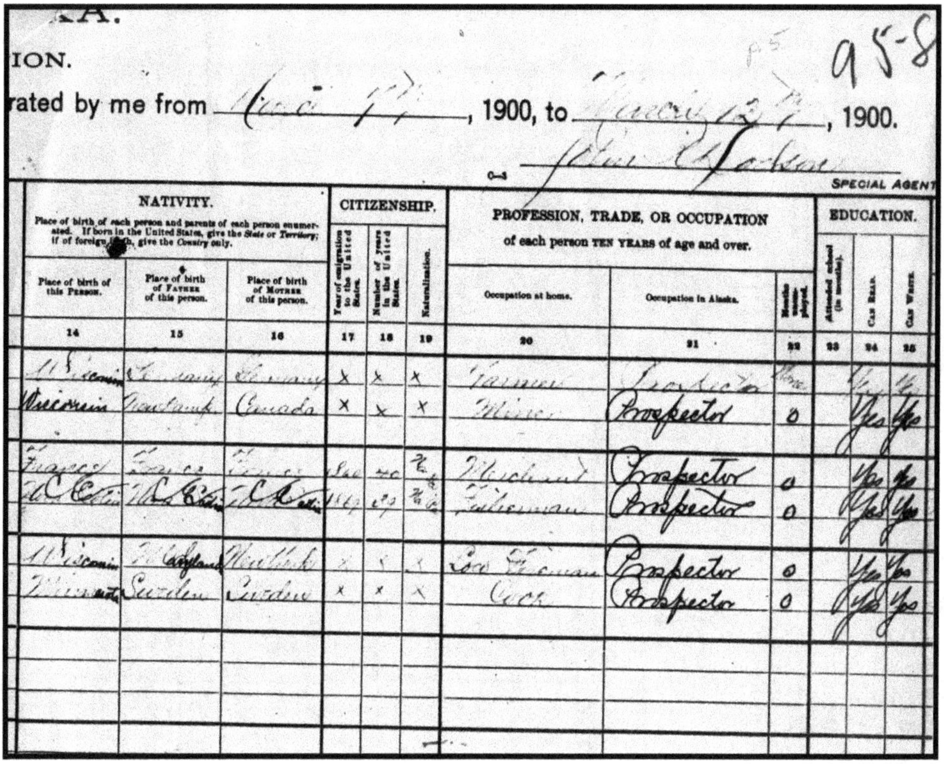

Census from Fort Independence. 1898

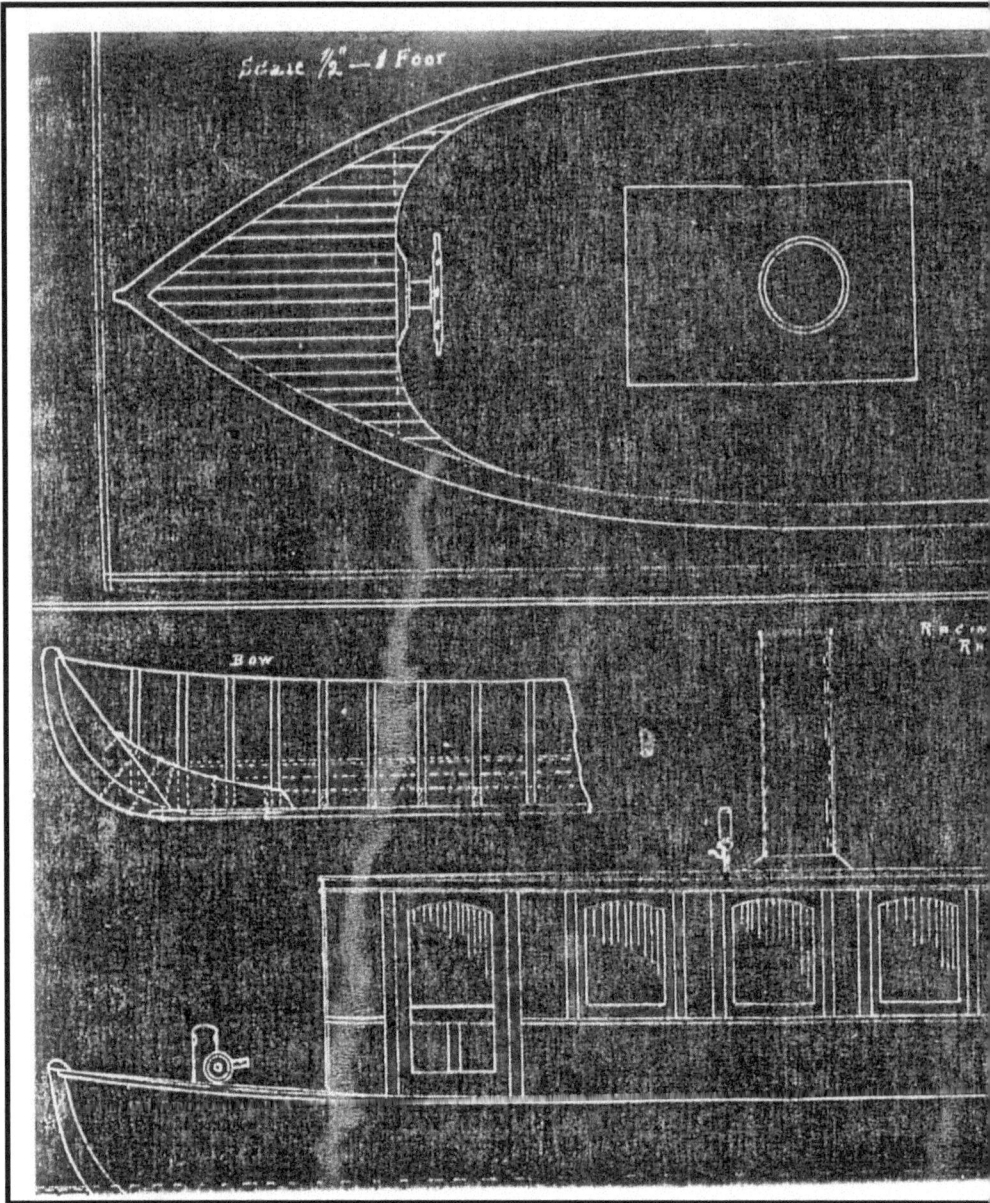

Scale ½" = 1 Foot

Bow

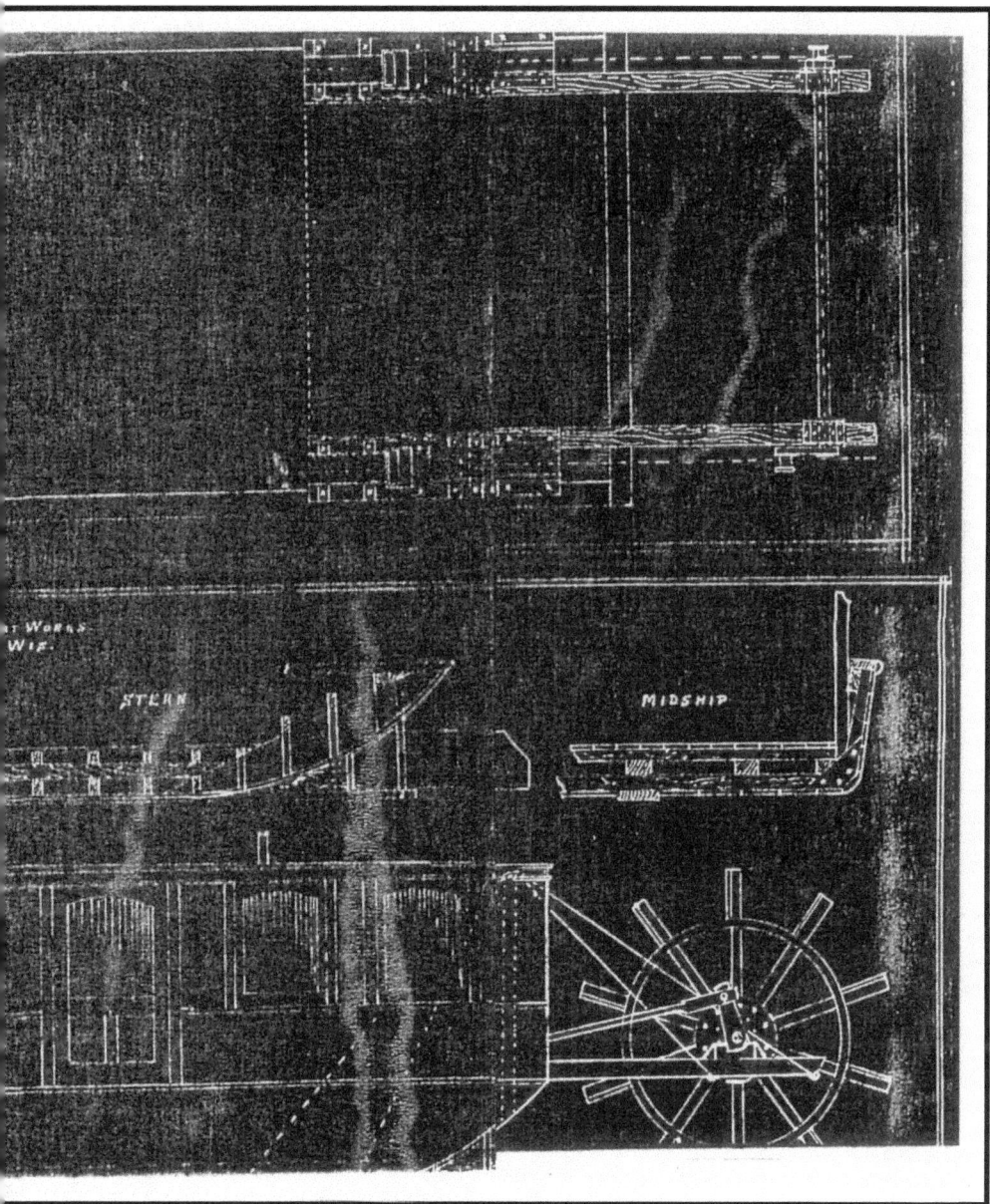

A "reduced" copy of the blueprint
of the Potlatch.

Fred Currier and dog Bella starting on prospecting trip on gulches of the Chena. 1899

www.ingramcontent.com/pod-product-compliance
Lightning Source LLC
Chambersburg PA
CBHW070753100426
42742CB00012B/2121